P9-DMH-984

PRAISE FOR PEACE SKILLS

"A must for people who want to be change agents in society. Addresses transformation of conflict from an empowerment perspective."—Craig Arendse, director of mediation and transformation practice, Cape Town, South Africa

"Offers a ray of hope for individuals and communities who long for peace and reconciliation."—Dr. G. Douglass Lewis, president, Wesley Theological Seminary

"JUSTPEACE chose this manual as its primary training text. . . . There is none better!"—Tom Porter, executive director, JUSTPEACE, United Methodist Church

"Peace Skills worked for me as a participant, and I depend on the Manual and Guide as a trainer."—Dr. William O'Brien, founding director, Global Center, Samford University and training coordinator for Birmingham Civil Rights Institute

"Enables individuals to engage conflict in a truly transformative manner. . . . The skills have proven effective in the formation of multicultural teams." —Michael Mata, director, Los Angeles Urban Leadership Institute and professor, urban studies, Claremont School of Theology

"This guide reminds us of the basic things we tend to forget: how to listen, how to be empathic to others, and how to see things from the perspective of others."—Christine Loh, member of Parliament and founder, Citizens Party in Hong Kong, China

"In Indonesia there is a great need to empower people for reconciliation. *Peace Skills* is just what we need. I have used the Leaders' Guide and

Manual in my training workshops at our center for Reconciliation and Peace and will use the Indonesian language translation even more."—Judo Poerwowidagdo, president, Krida Wacana University, Jakarta, Indonesia

"Invaluable resource . . . artfully blends 'the basics' with advanced approaches . . . beneficial to both first-time learners and experienced practitioners."—Dr. John Paul Lederach, professor, Conflict Transformation Program, Eastern Mennonite University

"The focus on community transformation and self-conscious reliance on spiritual and moral resources made the peace skills material distinctive. " —Dr. Thomas Hoyt, Bishop of CME church and former professor of New Testament at Howard University, ITC, and Hartford Seminary

"Our training has allowed Jacksonville to address issues in education, housing, and the environment. The program has equipped more than five hundred Jacksonville leaders to be agents of community transformation and has improved the quality and ownership of important public policy decisions." —Bill Scheu, lawyer and community leader, Jacksonville, Florida

PEACE
SKILLS

PEACE SKILLS

A MANUAL FOR COMMUNITY MEDIATORS

Ronald S. Kraybill with Robert A. Evans
and Alice Frazer Evans

JOSSEY-BASS
A Wiley Company
San Francisco

Copyright © 2001 by Jossey-Bass Inc., 350 Sansome Street, San Francisco, California 94104.

Jossey-Bass is a registered trademark of Jossey-Bass Inc., A Wiley Company.

The materials that appear in this book *(except those for which reprint permission must be obtained from the primary sources)* may be freely reproduced for educational/training activities. There is no requirement to obtain special permission for such uses. We do, however, ask that the following statement appear on all reproductions: *Peace Skills: A Manual for Community Mediators* by Ronald S. Kraybill with Alice Frazer Evans and Robert A. Evans. Copyright © 2001 by Jossey-Bass, San Francisco, CA.

This permission statement is limited to the reproduction of material for educational/training events. *Systematic or large-scale reproduction or distribution (more than one hundred copies per year)—or inclusion of items in publications for sale—may be done only with prior written permission. Also, reproduction on computer disk or by any other electronic means requires prior written permission. Please contact: Permissions Department, John Wiley & Sons, 605 Third Avenue, New York, NY 10158-0012.*

Jossey-Bass books and products are available through most bookstores. To contact Jossey-Bass directly, call (888) 378-2537, fax to (800) 605-2665, or visit our website at www.josseybass.com.

Substantial discounts on bulk quantities of Jossey-Bass books are available to corporations, professional associations, and other organizations. For details and discount information, contact the special sales department at Jossey-Bass.

Library of Congress Cataloging-in-Publication Data

Kraybill, Ronald S.
    Peace skills: a manual for community mediators / Ronald S. Kraybill with Alice Frazer Evans and Robert A. Evans.
        p. cm.
    Includes bibliographical references and index.
    ISBN 0-7879-4799-7 (alk. paper)
    1. Negotiation. 2. Mediation. 3. Conflict management. I. Evans, Alice F., date . II. Evans, Robert A., date . III. Title.
    BF637.N4 .K73 2000
    303.6'9—dc21   00-11082

PB Printing   10 9 8 7 6 5 4 3 2 1   FIRST EDITION

CONTENTS

ACKNOWLEDGMENTS

MANY PEOPLE helped bring this manual to print. The Mennonite Central Committee in Akron, Pennsylvania, was my institutional home from 1979 through 1988 and provided many opportunities to experiment, learn, and develop training exercises and materials in North America and other places. The Centre for Conflict Resolution in Cape Town, South Africa, provided an equally stimulating base from 1989 through 1995, during which time I served as director of training and director of special projects. Additional work was done from my current academic home at the Institute for Justice and Peacebuilding, Eastern Mennonite University, Harrisonburg, Virginia.

Empowering for Reconciliation with Justice, a South African coalition of organizations mandated to do conflict resolution training in religiously based settings, deserves thanks for providing financial support in converting what were previously sketchy training notes into a more accessible format. I owe special thanks to my collaborators Robert A. Evans and Alice Frazer Evans of Plowshares Institute, Simsbury, Connecticut, for their constant encouragement to persist, their vision for creating a comprehensive training packet, their editing skills, and their significant enrichment of these materials.

Several funders supported the completion of this training packet. These included the E. Rhodes and Leona B. Carpenter Foundation, the Ford Foundation, the William and Flora Hewlett Foundation, the James Irvine Foundation, the W. K. Kellogg Foundation, the John D. and Catherine T. MacArthur Foundation, and the Pew Charitable Trusts.

My greatest gratitude goes to the several thousand individuals who participated in workshops conducted over the past twenty years. In countless hours of "workshopping," sometimes exhilarating and sometimes painful, these participants taught me about conflict, about the many possibilities for responding to it, and about the art of leading a workshop that enables joint learning.

Ronald S. Kraybill
November 2000

INTRODUCTION

IT WAS TWO O'CLOCK in the morning. The Reverend Deric Solomon was sound asleep when he got a call from police in his hometown on the outskirts of Cape Town, South Africa. He later recalled, "Community people told the police I had some training in conflict resolution, so would I please come and help them." Solomon had just returned from a one-week workshop for community and religious leaders titled Empowering for Reconciliation with Justice.

Solomon's first thought was to say no. Praying for guidance, he deliberated what to do. In the darkness of his home, he fished out training materials and handwritten notes from the workshop. "As I went through the papers," he recalled, "I said to myself, 'This is something I can do.'" He drove to the address the police had given him and assisted in talking through a tense neighborhood situation. "I was a bit shaky," he remembered, "but my role helped make a difference."

The world is full of people like Deric Solomon, who was trusted as a leader deeply committed to his black and "coloured" (mixed-race) community. In every community reside people who are well connected to the struggles of life around them, respected for their involvement and abilities, and committed to peaceful resolution of painful conflicts. Unlike Solomon, however, most of these people have never had the opportunity to prepare for the task of building peace. Frequently unrecognized by others, often not confident in their own ability to make a contribution in tense environments, they represent a vast and underused resource for creative response to conflicts.

This manual is about preparing ordinary, involved community members like Deric Solomon to be peacebuilders. It arises from the experience of a growing number of people around the world who have discovered that peace does not happen through chance or wishful thinking but rather through faith, hard work, and planning. These people have discovered that they can learn and teach ideas and skills, which can make a difference in whether the conflicts in their families, organizations, and communities are constructive or destructive.

Life is full of conflict. The challenge is not to avoid it but rather to deal with conflict constructively, channeling the energy that conflict arouses in a positive direction so that just and life-giving change can take place. This understanding suggests a goal not of "resolving" or "managing" conflict but of *transforming* it. How does one go about drawing others into talking rather than fighting? How does one begin a meeting when people are tense and angry? How does one focus the discussions in such a way that people have the best chance of resolving the issues that divide them? How does one deal with deep wells of bitterness and resentment? If people have practical skills for dealing with these difficult moments, they can often direct the energy aroused by conflict to foster lasting and beneficial changes in the human community.

This manual is for people who want to improve their ability to handle conflict constructively in the places where they live and work. It is true that the world needs professional mediators and negotiators. However, there is a much greater need for skilled *laypeople*—ordinary leaders in families, neighborhoods, religious bodies, and community and political organizations who can help others work out their differences on a daily basis.

The focus of the manual is on mediating, on standing between two or more parties in conflict and trying to assist them through their conflicts. However, anyone who thoughtfully explores this volume will discover that mediation skills have an extraordinary carryover. As one workshop participant put it, "I thought I was coming to a workshop on mediation skills. I didn't realize it would transform my personal relationships." Someone else said, "Mediating is not only about making peace; it gives us skills for strengthening communities and organizations and helps us build coalitions with others in the struggle for justice." Peacebuilders can bring a constructive "mediating presence" to conflict situations on many more occasions than when they engage in formal mediation.

Why should people get involved in a feud if it puts their own peace at risk? What sustains people like Deric Solomon, when they find themselves absorbing the anger and even hatred of adversaries? What enables a peacebuilder to have hope when long-sought agreements begin to fall apart? Where do people get the motivation, energy, sustaining commitment, and enduring hope to become peacebuilders and agents of conflict transformation?

This book focuses on *skill,* but for the authors, hope that endures must rest on a deeper foundation. Faith in a God who hungers for justice and peace has carried us into difficult circumstances to attempt things that may appear futile. We believe that God's presence and grace allow restoration of broken relationships, enable reform of unjust structures, and provide spiritual and moral guidance toward a better future for people wounded by the past. While we are sustained and guided by our Christian faith, we also see that a variety of religious traditions and moral mandates motivate others to pursue the path to peace with justice. Thus we have sought to present ideas in ways that are useful to and respectful of people from many backgrounds.

OVERVIEW OF THE MANUAL

This manual has three purposes

1. It is the foundation for a training workshop in conflict transformation using mediation skills.

2. It provides additional reading for workshop participants wishing to extend and deepen their learnings.

3. It offers ideas for solitary readers who wish to learn more about mediation and conflict transformation.

The chapters follow the order in which much of the material is introduced in a workshop. Section One identifies our assumptions about conflict, about responding to conflict constructively, and about the nature of conflict. These assumptions have shaped both the content and the specific approaches to peacebuilding highlighted in the manual. Section Two focuses on mediation. This section suggests ways to initiate dialogue between conflicting parties and proposes a four-stage mediation process. Section Three contains chapters on special skills such as paraphrasing, attention to language, and dealing with emotions in conflict situations. These special skills apply to all stages of mediation. Section Four extends the values and skills of mediation in individual conflict to work in group conflicts. The focus of this section is on principles of good process design.

Throughout the manual, readers will find individual and small group exercises to help them develop greater self-awareness of their own approaches to conflict and to practice the skills identified in each chapter.

Should only experienced conflict transformation trainers conduct workshops on peacebuilding? Not necessarily. The need for training in conflict transformation skills at all levels of society is so vast that communities cannot afford to limit leadership of training to professional trainers. Besides,

Thoughts About Peace and Transformation

"It hath been told thee, O Man, what is good, and what the Lord doth require of thee; only to do justly, and to love mercy, and to walk humbly with thy God."

Torah: Micah 6:8

"And if they incline to peace, then incline to it and trust Allah; surely He is the Hearing, the Knowing."

Qur'an: The Accessions 8:61

"Blessed are the Peacemakers, for they shall be called the children of God."

Christian New Testament: Matthew 5:9

"Violence as a way of achieving racial justice is both impractical and immoral. It is impractical because it is a descending spiral ending in destruction for all. The old law of an eye for an eye leaves everybody blind. It is immoral because it seeks to humiliate the opponent rather than win his understanding; it seeks to annihilate rather then convert. Violence is immoral because it thrives on hatred rather than love. It destroys community and makes brotherhood impossible. It leaves society in monologue rather than dialogue. Violence ends by defeating itself. It creates bitterness in the survivors and brutality in the destroyers."

Martin Luther King Jr., Stride Toward Freedom

"Mediation has the potential to do far more than create agreements and improve relationships. It has the potential to transform people's lives, to give them both an increased sense of their own personal efficacy (empowerment) and a greater openness to and acceptance of the person seated on the other side of the table (recognition). Even if no agreement is reached, even if no reconciliation results, mediation should still be regarded as a success if it brings empowerment and recognition. And if agreement is reached as well, so much the better."

Robert A. Baruch Bush and Joseph P. Folger,
The Promise of Mediation

the best workshops center not on the wisdom of the trainer but on the collective insights of the participants. Rather than declaring *"the* way" to address conflict, this manual is written to encourage community peacebuilders to learn from one another the most effective ways to approach different situations.

This volume does not begin to capture the richness of insight that emerges in even one three-day gathering of twenty people committed to advancing their skills in peacebuilding. But we hope it inspires others who share the vision that has brought thousands of people in South Africa, Asia, North America, and many other places to participate in conflict transformation. Like Deric Solomon, these ordinary people are the world's best prospect for peace. Their work offers a hopeful glimpse of the future: a world where diversity and conflict no longer divide but instead serve as potent energizers of human encounter and the struggle for justice.

PEACE SKILLS

Section One

Assumptions About Conflict and the Role of Peacebuilders

CHAPTER 1

Assumptions About Conflict

CONFLICT PRESENTS US with choices that form our destiny, choices that both reflect and shape who we are as persons and communities. These choices go beyond the immediate issues in dispute. They mold our hearts and alter the world in which our children and grandchildren will live. In moments of conflict, we make long-lasting decisions about the institutions and resources with which we construct our lives. Our deepest values shape and are shaped by our choices. Few moments bring together so many far-reaching choices as the moment of conflict. Thus we do well to pay attention to it. How we respond in conflict will either limit us or open the way to life in abundance.

The Chinese character for *crisis* or *conflict* is composed of two symbols, one meaning "danger" and the other meaning "opportunity":

Conflict is dangerous. Every hour of every day, people die as a result of conflict in our world. One reason conflict is so dangerous is that human beings have invested lavishly in one particular response to it: the technology and application of violence. Everyone knows that to prevail in war, it is necessary to invest in weapons and train vigorously in their use. Most nations spend more money on "national defense" than on education, health care, and all other human services combined.

Military academies abound, but what about people and places equipped to assist in peaceful resolution of conflicts? How many people do you know who have invested so much as an hour of conscious effort in learning skills for constructive, nonviolent ways of responding to conflict? If we practice and prepare for the use of violence, we will reap violence. If we want peace, we must begin to practice and prepare in the arts of peace.

Conflict is also opportunity. Every day, women and men choose to confront destructive words and actions in ways that encourage positive change. Every day, people in organizations and groups discuss serious differences with others and find creative ways of dealing with diversity. These efforts may be accompanied by conflict, but it is conflict waged in a way that strengthens the human community.

If we wish to improve life for our children, our communities, and ourselves, we should not run from all conflict. If we instead recognize that good can come from conflict and if we equip ourselves with skills to respond transformatively, we can direct the energy of conflict away from destruction into opportunities for constructive change. Skills can never guarantee success, but they can greatly increase our chances of good outcomes. When we prepare ourselves with the necessary skills, we find that many conflicts can strengthen the human community, bringing new levels of involvement, new awareness, new patterns of relationship, and even justice itself.

CONFLICT TRANSFORMATION

What words should we use to describe work in conflict? The question is important, because our words indicate much about our understanding of the context in which we operate and what we seek to do there. "My goal is conflict prevention! Why waste time responding to conflict if you can prevent it?" said a senior executive in a workshop. "Conflict prevention" is a worthy goal; so long as it includes addressing the realities of injustice that often underlie conflict. But the concept is ambiguous. Leaders of black communities in South Africa in the 1980s were not interested in preventing conflict. They had very good reasons for wanting to stir it up!

The expression "conflict management" was widely used in business and organization settings in the 1980s. But can anybody really "manage" conflict? Can geologists "manage" Mount Vesuvius? Must we "manage" the sun to benefit from solar energy? In the 1990s, the expression "conflict resolution" gained acceptance in business, community, and religious settings. But the same reservations about "conflict prevention" apply here. Some conflicts ought not to be resolved.

In this manual, we will speak of "conflict transformation," for it suggests that the goal is not only to *end or prevent* something bad but also to *begin* something new and good. Transformation asserts the belief that conflict can be a catalyst for deep-rooted, enduring, positive change in individuals, relationships, and the structures of the human community. Alongside stories of pain and destruction, history offers stories of profound change for the good taking place in response to conflict. Religious history in particular contains powerful stories of change resulting from conflict. People in crisis sometimes take a new look at themselves and do not like what they see. This awareness opens the way for profound change from the core of their being. In Christian scriptures, Zaccheus, the hated tax collector, seeks out Jesus, who angers onlookers by requesting to stay at Zaccheus' house. Zaccheus is so moved that he announces he will give half his belongings to the poor and repay fourfold those he has cheated.

Most mediators recognize that something more than merely "resolving a conflict" often takes place in mediation. Disputants may pass through moments of soul-searching and engagement with each other that are rare in normal living. Discovery and hope sometimes flow so strongly that mediators themselves feel renewed. These moments occur just often enough that some mediators speak in awed voices of the terrain between parties as "holy ground." No techniques can guarantee that our work will transform the landscape of conflict from earth into holy ground. But by calling our work "conflict transformation," we signal awareness of important possibilities: human beings and the communities in which we live *can* change for the better. Conflict offers unusual moments of opportunity for such change. As peacebuilders, we seek to assist in gaining maximum change for the better from moments of conflict.

How can we assist these changes? In part by giving opportunity for things to happen between the parties that are often overlooked. Conflict transformation recognizes that our humanity is measured not by wealth or material status but by how we manage the abilities and talents given to us, how we relate to those who trouble us, how we respond to the rich and ever-unfolding mysteries of life. Conflict transformation works in the nitty-gritty realities of material issues, but with an eye to the deeper questions at stake.

At the heart of conflict transformation lies profound respect for the value and uniqueness of every human being. Mediators function transformatively by seeking to foster awareness of this intrinsic worth within each party. Two particular strategies deserve special attention here. On the one hand, transformative mediators actively seek to assist parties in reaching for their fullest potential as human beings. Mediators do this by interacting with parties in ways that encourage healthy selfhood; by inviting them to formulate and express their preferences, hopes, needs, and dreams; by assisting them in exploring all possible options in attaining that which they seek; and by expecting them to take responsibility for their own lives and problems. Some mediators call this strategy *empowerment*.[1]

A second transformative strategy is to expand the parties' capacity to recognize and accept the value and dignity of others. Mediators do this by modeling respect for others in their own conduct, by providing guidelines and frameworks for conversation that support civility, by giving each party opportunities to hear and encounter the experiences of the other party, by noting and highlighting commonalties between the parties, by facilitating joint problem solving, by providing opportunities for parties to acknowledge errors and mend relationships, and so forth. Some mediators call this strategy *recognition.*

When the needs of self conflict with the needs of others, people commonly choose one response and abandon the other: they focus on empowerment of self and abandon recognition of others, or they recognize the needs of others at the expense of empowerment of self. Maintaining active commitment to *both* is a challenge to mind and heart.

From the perspective of conflict transformation, when human beings are able to meet this challenge, changes take place that are more significant than settling a feud. Engaging in these dual activities makes us better people; it improves our ability to live well and create a world in which others can live well. Although the conflict may be about material matters, our responses to it can change us morally and spiritually. It is this deeper level of change that is of greatest interest for a transformative mediator. Of course, no human being is ever completely empowered, nor is anyone ever able to fully appreciate the intrinsic worth of others. Thus the goal of transformation serves more as a guiding beacon than as a result that is fully attained in a mediation session. But the criterion for success is *not* whether or not "settlement" has been reached. Rather, it is whether or not people in conflict have changed and grown in ways that make them better people. More specifically, it is whether or not they have made practical choices that expand their ability to fulfill their potential as human beings and at the same time honor the worth and dignity of others.

THE ROLE OF PEACEBUILDERS

The concept of conflict transformation implies that human beings are not doomed to endless repetition of historical hostilities. It is possible to respond in new, unexpected ways that break patterns of destructive behavior and end cycles of retaliation. However, for this to happen requires imagining possibilities that go beyond mere "conflict management" or "dispute resolution." Someone must be present with a vision for more than securing grudging agreements, who sees the possibilities for growth and development within each party, for increased respect and tolerance of others, for restored relationships and reworking of unjust structures.

That person must further understand that transformation requires change not only from without but also from within. Change that is purely coerced is not transformation; it is merely adjustment to force. Forced change can lead to opportunities for the kind of reflective encounter required for transformation, but unless that encounter takes place, coercion only polarizes and separates people without bringing real change. As soon as the coercion is gone, things revert to old, destructive patterns that are stronger than ever.

Conflict transformation places paradoxical demands on those committed to facilitating it. On one hand, it requires a clear, unwavering commitment to assist others to grow and change in their journey toward reaching their fullest potential and to honor that potential in others. On the other hand, it requires careful self-management to maintain the facilitative, invitational stance essential to the possibility of transformation.

We call such persons peacebuilders. Peacebuilders recognize that peace is built over time, through processes of encounter and reflection that address not only practical issues of conflict but also deeper issues of relationships, human development, and structural realities. They see in conflict more than the sparks of friction between unchangeable opposites. They see, rather, a fire that is capable of transforming the people generating the heat. Peacebuilders seek to be a long-term presence that helps harness the energy of conflict and directs it positively to change and renew the human community.

If the only thing peacebuilders are concerned about is to bring an end to conflict, they may do more harm than good. For example, if peacebuilders achieve "peace" without the parties' addressing the causes of their conflict and their own role in maintaining those causes, peacebuilders may only prolong the day when essential issues are finally addressed. Where people are blocked from expressing their views and disagreements, resentment and frustration grow and fester. Usually it is just a matter of time before these negative emotions erupt. Thus a major goal is to create channels and structures that make it possible for people to express their concerns and feelings in appropriate ways. When substantial power inequalities exist, a critical challenge for peacebuilders is to enable weaker parties to express their concerns without unwisely endangering them. Sometimes peacebuilding efforts create the appearance that the conflict is only getting worse, for one result is often an increase in expressions of different viewpoints. However, as people recognize that room will be given to voice their concerns, they often become more constructive in the ways they interact with each other.

Peacebuilders operate in ways that contribute to the human development of the people involved in conflict. Throughout this manual, peacebuilders are called to relate to the parties in ways that increase the parties' ability to consider their options and take an active role in making decisions themselves rather than have them made by others. If peacebuilders work carefully to empower people in this way, they make a fundamental contribution to justice, for they equip people to participate in their own liberation from the situations and structures that oppress and dehumanize them. This approach to conflict requires time, careful analysis, planning, and a variety of strategies. The manual refers to this full set of activities as *peacebuilding*.

RESOURCES FOR PEACEBUILDERS

As suggested in the Introduction, we, like many other peacebuilders, believe that spiritual and moral resources provide a foundation for peacebuilding. The ability to work for change and for just peace is not merely an accomplishment of will and skill. It is a gift from the very source of life itself. Many faith-based traditions affirm that God, addressed by many names, grants reconciliation as a gift. The healing of a relationship, the restoration of a community, and the resurrection of hope come through God's loving care for divided children. Peacebuilders become agents of reconciliation and healing by becoming channels of God's restoring action. This means that assisting others to use conflict as an opportunity to transform relationships and empower them to build just and stable communities becomes a way of life.

We must acknowledge that spiritual and moral resources have been frequently employed in ways that promote division, hatred, and violence. Religious factions have distorted these resources to fuel alienation, not reconciliation. However, the majority of the world's great spiritual and moral traditions give priority to reconciliation with justice. These traditions also emphasize the values of empowerment and liberation. The parties to a conflict do not need to share the same spiritual and moral convictions as the peacebuilders for the peacebuilding process to succeed. However, the ability to draw on moral and spiritual resources can restore and revitalize all peacebuilders in their work of mediation and reconciliation. We believe that the neglect of these resources has been a significant loss to strife-torn communities around the world.

THE NORMALITY OF CONFLICT

One place to begin learning how to deal constructively with conflict is with attitudes toward it. When people believe that conflict is wrong, a sign of failure, and inevitably destructive, they feel threatened or defensive when serious differences arise. This sense of fear and threat quickly creates a self-fulfilling prophecy. Rather than talk openly with others, people who are afraid or ashamed of conflict begin avoiding them, and relationships are weakened as a consequence. Increasingly, people choose either "fight or flight"; that is, rather than constructively engaging others, they choose the extreme options of either becoming aggressive or withdrawing from communication.

If people accept that conflict is normal, it is easier to maintain good relationships with those they disagree with. If they take the attitude that conflict is capable of bringing changes that can strengthen them and their community, the chances are higher that the conflict will indeed bring constructive outcomes.

A VARIETY OF APPROACHES

There is no "right" way to address conflicts. The focus of this manual is on facilitating direct, face-to-face discussion between parties in conflict. It would be wrong, however, to assume that this is the only way to deal with conflict. A community leader from Malaysia suggested how he would deal with conflict in his community:

> *In my rural community of Malaysian Chinese, to openly state differences with another person is considered rude. Bringing two people together, face to face, to talk about their conflict would only make things worse, and they would probably be even more upset afterward. To be polite, they would probably feel that they have no choice but to deny that there is any problem. When I am trying to assist others in solving a problem, I go to one party alone and talk. Then I go to the other party. However, I am careful, so careful that the second person may not even realize that the first person is unhappy. It might require many such meetings over a long period until the problem is sorted out.*

Some strategies described in this manual could make conflicts in such a community worse, not better. Every community is different, with its own history and culture. What works well in one place may not work in another, or it may work only with significant adaptation. This requires us to view learning about more effective responses to conflict as a conversation. In this conversation, people present their ideas of how to respond to conflict, compare these with other ideas, and test strategies in role-play or real-life settings.

However, in the end, we must all make our own choices about effective responses for the communities in which we live.

This manual offers one voice in such a conversation. As a way of inviting dialogue, it begins with assumptions and basic beliefs about conflict that undergird the ideas presented. Although the authors have extensive international experience, we were raised in Anglo-European communities in North America and are deeply influenced by this context. We hope that making our basic assumptions transparent will make it easier for readers to look at themselves and their own context. What are your own assumptions about conflict? What will work in responding to conflicts in your community? This manual cannot answer these questions, but if it helps you find your own answers, it will accomplish its purpose.

APPLICATION EXERCISES

Thinking about personal assumptions and attitudes about conflict is a fruitful place to begin your side of the conversation. If you have a negative attitude toward all conflict in all settings, your behavior in conflict is more likely to be extreme. On one hand, you may be too nice, too accommodating, and hence subject to exploitation. On the other, a negative attitude towards conflict may cause you to be judgmental, harsh, and inflexible when challenged. The following exercises may help you think more deeply about your attitudes toward conflict.

1. Do this exercise in two parts. Read part (b) only after you have done part (a).

   a. Without censoring your thoughts, write down words you think of when you think of conflict. Stop when you have a list of eight to fifteen words.

   b. Examine your list. Are all of your words negative? Is conflict always a bad thing? Does anything positive ever come from conflict? What is the difference between constructive and destructive conflict?

      A third part of this exercise could involve considering all the positive effects of a past conflict.

2. Ask a friend to join you in this exercise. Discuss the following questions.

   a. How did my parents or the people I grew up with deal with conflict? (Did they avoid it, accommodate at all cost, take rigid positions, or flexibly and creatively seek solutions acceptable to all?) How did I deal with conflict in that family?

b. What are the primary ways I deal with conflict today?

Recall concrete situations that illustrate your response to each of these questions.

3. Think about a specific time when you were willing and able to stand between two or more people in conflict and try to help them deal with their differences. What were your reasons for intervening? Where did your strength come from to become a mediating presence in this situation?

CHAPTER 2

Understanding Conflict
and the Role of Mediation

THE WORD *CONFLICT* comes from the Latin *confligere*, which means "to strike or clash together." Two dry sticks continuously struck together will frequently lead to a fire.

The "fire" created by conflicts is not necessarily destructive. There are times when genuine peacebuilders are deeply involved in creating conflict. Conflicts created in the southern United States in the 1960s by nonviolent bus boycotts led to the repeal of unjust discrimination laws. The conflicts created by Mahatma Gandhi's active nonviolence crusade ultimately freed India from British colonial rule. Conflicts stirred by the anti-apartheid movement in South Africa eventually led to constructive change in that nation's governmental structure. A critical difference between a destructive and a constructive conflict is how the conflict is addressed, especially whether or not the parties have the skills—and will—to use the conflict to move toward constructive change.

The daily news is filled with examples of destructive conflicts, ranging from international warfare to community and personal confrontations. Most people experience some form of conflict every day, either in their family, at work, or in their community. These conflicts usually occur when two or more people believe they have irreconcilable differences or feel that their resources, relationships, needs, or values are threatened. People clash when they are unable to work out these differences and so respond to one another in destructive ways.

RESPONSES TO CONFLICT

People respond to conflict in varied ways. One person will retreat into silence; another will openly confront; a third will begin to negotiate. The same person may respond differently to different types of conflict. These reactions arise not only from the nature of specific conflicts but also from personal history, which deeply shapes each person's attitudes and beliefs about conflict. Influences that have special impact include:

- Relationships with siblings and childhood friends
- Responses to conflict modeled by parents, teachers, and public figures
- Images and attitudes presented by public media, especially television, movies, and the Internet
- Social factors such as serious deprivation and poverty

The first and most important step toward handling conflict well is for people to become aware of their spontaneous and often unconscious reactions to conflict and the effects of their responses on others.

Before reading further, reflect on the following sets of questions:

1. In conflicts in which I am involved,
   - How do I usually respond to conflicts?
   - Where did these patterns come from (family, friends, life experience)?
   - How do my responses affect other people?

2. When I try to facilitate a constructive approach or mediate in a dispute between other people,
   - What responses on my part seem to block the people involved?
   - What responses seem to help people talk about their real issues and work out their problems?

3. When I consider a goal of being a peacebuilder,
   - What values inform my desire to be a peacebuilder? What are the sources of these values?
   - Am I willing to change my own patterns of response that are destructive or disempowering?
   - How will I begin to learn about these patterns?

Greater self-understanding is an important step toward constructive, alternative responses. Responding honestly to these questions can lead to new insights about your reactions to conflict and your feelings and beliefs about peacebuilding. Asking for and accepting honest feedback from colleagues will also greatly increase your understanding.

This manual contains suggestions of numerous approaches that peacebuilders have found effective. However, *becoming a peacebuilder is more than learning new skills and techniques; it is a way of life.* Peacebuilding comes from a deep place in the heart. It grows from genuine concern, love, and acceptance of other people. Even when you do not agree with other people, you will be challenged to empathize with them, to step into their world, and to understand their perspective and their feelings.

Peacebuilding often means becoming the bridge between people who are unwilling or unable to speak to one another. Emotional reactions may cloud their ability to understand a conflict situation with any degree of objectivity. Consequently, as a peacebuilder, you are also frequently challenged to bring clear and objective analysis to a conflict situation. The following section offers some ways to think about conflict objectively.

SOURCES AND TYPES OF CONFLICT

There are many ways to analyze the nature of a conflict and to identify the factors that "cause" or contribute to it. Although there may be one precipitating event that brings opponents into confrontation, most conflicts, particularly those in communities, arise from a complex set of factors that include the particular people involved; the history these people share; the dynamics of the social, political, or economic environment; and the specific issues about which people disagree. In one community, for example, a school board conflict appeared to be about a pending vote to purchase metal detectors for a high school with funds previously set aside for long-term school reform. However, the community mediator found that many other factors had to be considered in order to address this conflict constructively—fears expressed by teachers about school safety, economic instability in the community, racial tensions on the school board and in the community, issues of power on the school board and in the community, and so forth.

Often it is helpful to approach a conflict by assessing the nature of the issues at stake. Conflicts usually arise from one or several of the following matters:

- Information
- Resources
- Relationships
- Interests or needs
- Structures (social or organizational)
- Values

yes!

Many conflicts involve a combination of these areas or even all of them. By analyzing and identifying the specific areas involved, a complex conflict can become easier to manage. Conflicts about information or over resources may be easier to resolve than conflicts over relationships or interests. The latter are usually easier to resolve than conflicts over structures. Conflicts over values are often the most difficult to resolve because they involve the things people hold most dear—the beliefs that shape their identity and faith perspectives that give meaning to their lives.

For example, the school board mediator found that additional *information* about the cost of metal detectors and locating other funding *(resources)* addressed the immediate crisis. However, peacebuilding, which addressed long-term needs of the school board, ultimately required dealing with more personal *interests* of board members and even the reorganization of some of the committee *structures.* By building more trusting relationships, board members came to greater tolerance of one another's *values.*

Conflicts About Information

In many instances, the parties do not have sufficient information, or even the same information, about a situation. Collecting and clarifying facts can go a long way toward easing tensions. In other situations, parties interpret the data in differing ways or assign different levels of importance to the same data. Open discussion and input from trusted outside consultants can help in assessing the relevance of available information.

Conflicts over Resources

Conflicts about material resources such as land, money, or objects are normally obvious to identify and often lend themselves well to straightforward bargaining. Sometimes, however, although the parties appear to be squabbling over a resource, the real conflict is about something else, perhaps relationships or psychological needs of one or both parties.

Conflicts over Relationships

People in family relationships, business partnerships, or community organizations commonly have disagreements over a variety of specific issues, but sometimes the interdependence created by their relationship introduces a destructive dimension to differences that would otherwise find easy resolution. Events of the past or years of stereotyping may make people inflexible or unwilling to try even the most fair and obvious solution. Clarity regarding goals, roles, responsibilities, and different perspectives about past experiences may need to be addressed before the other conflicts can be tackled.

Conflicts over Interests or Needs

Important and powerful human needs for such things as identity, respect, or participation are often at the heart of conflicts that appear to be contests for material things. Constructive opportunities for individuals and communities to express their needs and feel that they have been heard are critical to addressing these needs. Often long-term resolution of a conflict that is focused on resources depends as much on meeting the interests or needs of the people involved as on dividing the resources.

Conflicts About Structures

Social and organizational structures determine who has access to power or resources, who is afforded respect, and who has authority to make decisions. Conflicts about or within structures often involve issues of justice and competing goals. Such conflicts often require years of effort to effect constructive change.[1]

Conflicts Involving Values

Values and beliefs are formed by life experiences and faith perspectives. Because a challenge to a person's values is often seen as a threat to one's identity, conflicts involving values are usually the most difficult to resolve. Most people react defensively to this threat and withdraw from any negotiation, assuming that resolution of the conflict will require changing their values. But in reality, being able to clarify their values and feel that they have been heard and understood often allows parties to move away from defensiveness and even learn to live together in mutual acknowledgment of their differences.

Summary

Attempting to understand a conflict by considering the people involved, its history, social setting, issues, and a variety of causal or contributing factors can be liberating for both the peacebuilder and the parties. This process helps break a complex conflict down into more manageable parts and opens the door to a variety of approaches to resolution.

APPROACHES TO ADDRESSING CONFLICT

Individuals and communities deal with conflict in a variety of ways. A common approach in many cultures is simply to *avoid conflict* whenever possible. At the other extreme is the tendency to respond with *violence*. Between these extremes, most societies have developed structured approaches to addressing actual and potential conflicts between individuals and among groups or communities.

People who choose to face a conflict might begin by simply discussing the issues. They may then decide to move to a process of *negotiation* about one or more specific issues. If they feel they are not able to work out an agreement, they may decide to bring in a third person to assist them. The initial role of this "third party" may be as a *conciliator,* one who simply focuses on reducing hostility. If the parties feel they need additional help, they may use a *mediator,* who actively assists them in exploring options and negotiating a settlement. A mediator avoids imposing decisions and helps the parties find mutually acceptable solutions. If mediation fails, or as an alternative to it, the parties might involve an *arbitrator,* who assumes the responsibility for making a decision. Unlike mediation, arbitration is a form of adjudication; like a judge, an arbitrator decides right and wrong and imposes a decision. The court system, which includes judges and juries, is a more formal type of adjudication, with complex procedures and rules of evidence. Government bodies, which develop legislation, also provide effective means for addressing areas of conflict or potential conflict. Like judges and juries, legislation places responsibility and authority for decisions in the hands of a third party.

At any point in the conflict, parties may move to avoidance or violence. However, although avoidance is common as an initial response, parties rarely return to it after they have chosen an active response, and they are unlikely to resort to violence if they believe other responses are available to meet their needs. With the exception of violence, each response deserves consideration according to the situation, the issues, and the people involved in the conflict. However, as Figure 2.1 suggests, the farther along the spectrum one moves, the less control the parties have over their decisions. This is particularly true when parties cross the "legal due-process boundary" between mediation and arbitration.

This manual focuses on only one of these approaches—mediation. Particularly when cultural, ethnic, and social differences make direct negotiation difficult or impossible, mediation may be the most constructive way to address community conflicts. Mediation provides a "safe" way for the parties to come together while allowing them to maintain control over the issues, the relationships, and the outcome. Mediation has the potential for transformation and peacebuilding by helping the parties in three ways:

- Mediation helps them gain greater understanding of each other's needs, interests, and values.

- Mediation helps them take responsibility for the decisions they make.

- Mediation may lay the groundwork to change their relationship and begin working together to share resources, clarify information, and even change structures that may have been a source of conflict.

FIGURE 2.1. Approaches to Handling Conflict.

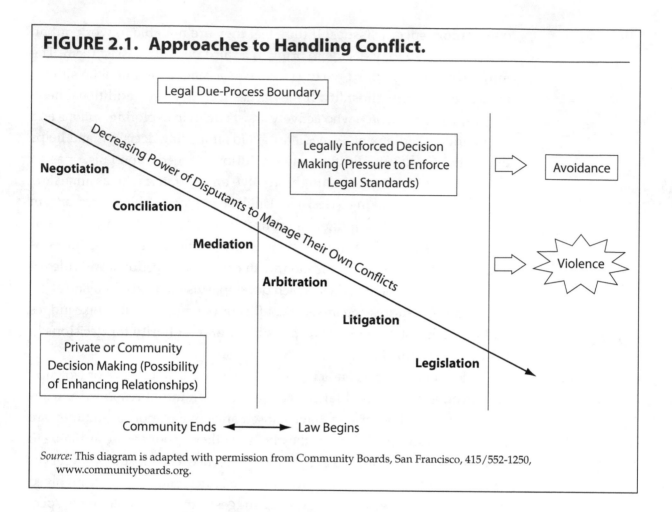

Source: This diagram is adapted with permission from Community Boards, San Francisco, 415/552-1250, www.communityboards.org.

THE LIMITS OF MEDIATION

Conflict transformation recognizes that peace and justice are one. Peace without justice is not true peace. Justice without peace cannot endure. Conflict transformation approaches every situation of conflict with eyes on both commitments.

Because mediation is such an essential and adaptable skill, and because it is impossible to confront injustice effectively without the coalition-building capacities that the mediation process provides, this manual focuses primarily on mediation as a peacebuilding response. However, there is danger in this. People who are overly enthusiastic about mediation can damage important efforts of others or discredit their own work if they fail to recognize the limits of mediation. Imagine the following situations:

- What if Rosa Parks had chosen to mediate her conflict with the bus driver in Montgomery rather than refuse to move out of her seat?

- What if South African blacks had chosen to enter mediation with the apartheid government about political rights in the most intense period of oppression between 1950 and 1990?

- What if a property owner routinely mistreats and cheats tenants, who all choose to limit their responses to individual mediation sessions, thereby permitting the owner to continue his abuse of other unknowing tenants?

- What if a pastor or counselor makes sexual advances to a client in a counseling session and friends advise the client to do nothing more than have a mediation session with the offender?

- What if a wife is being physically abused by her husband and her family encourages her to suffer in silence?

[The pattern common to these situations is that (1) one party holds significant relational, institutional, or structural power over the other party and (2) the powerful party has engaged in activities that are clearly *unjust* or *unethical.*]Whenever these factors are present, there is reason for caution about the use of mediation. Efforts to bring the parties into negotiation without careful attention to the readiness of the stronger party to clearly acknowledge wrongdoing and the preparedness of weaker party to confront the stronger without being merely silenced are likely to cause more harm than good. [Peacebuilders should ensure that supporters and advocates of justice are available to the weaker party to assist in the balancing of power before proceeding with exploration of talks.]In some cases mediation should not be considered until a lengthy stage of preparation and equalizing of power has taken place.

JUSTICE AND "NEUTRALITY"

Another challenge for peacebuilders dealing with issues of injustice is the idea that they should always be neutral. "The church calls us to be agents of reconciliation," explained a church leader about a community conflict. "That means we must be neutral and avoid taking sides." In another situation, responding to concerns raised by community leaders about violence initiated by one party to an ongoing mediation, a mediator said, "Yes, I am aware of the recent attacks. But we are trying to make peace here, and that means we must maintain our neutrality. I cannot comment at this time."

These comments are misguided. Neutrality is never a necessary or constructive goal in conflict, particularly in relation to issues of justice. In fact, talk of "neutrality" has caused much injury to the cause of peacebuilding. It confuses many mediators with a false understanding of their task and blocks many sincere leaders from acting on their own deeply held principles of justice. It also damages the credibility of peacemakers in general because it suggests that they do not have values or do not really care about what happens to people in conflict.

Neutrality is an illusion; there is no such thing as a detached or objective observer. Natural and social scientists have in recent years come to recognize this as a fact both in the natural world and the social world. For example, even if observers sit in a corner in complete silence while two people fight, their mere silence communicates certain things to the fighters—"Hitting is an acceptable way to resolve differences," or "This conflict has no significance for me," or even "I approve of what is happening" might be the message implied by their silence.

If we are not neutral, what are we? It helps in answering the question if we recognize there are several kinds of advocacy. *Party advocates* support one party, regardless of the issues. *Issue advocates* support whoever agrees with their views of a particular issue. *Process advocates* promote neither a particular party nor a favored point of view, but rather a particular approach to negotiation or decision making. Mediators cannot advocate a particular party or point of view, but we can and often must advocate particular processes for making decisions. We advocate processes that uphold the dignity and equality of the people involved, involve all people affected by a decision in the decision-making process itself, give all participants equal access to information, ensure that participants are fully informed about their legal rights, and hold parties accountable for their commitments. Mediators need not necessarily "take sides" in order to serve these values, but we should actively and openly encourage methods of talking that reflect them. We should also be prepared to walk away, if necessary, from a mediation role in situations that erode the values we stand for, so our skills are not used for purposes we oppose. Rather than being "neutral," peacebuilders should seek to be impartial, fair, principled, and committed to the legitimate needs of all. A variety of terms can be used to describe our role, but we should avoid a description that robs us of the heart of our identity and values.

 For additional material on addressing justice issues in group and intergroup conflicts, see "Guidelines for a Just Peace in Community Conflicts" at www.josseybass.com/peaceskills.

APPLICATION EXERCISES

1. With a partner, choose a specific personal or community conflict, and explore the following aspects:

   a. Identify the people involved as well as elements of history, context, and specific issues that contributed to the conflict.

   b. Determine the impact of the following matters on the conflict: resources, information or misinformation, relationships among people, their specific interests or needs, organizational and systemic structures, and values held by people involved in the conflict.

   c. What have you learned about the conflict from this discussion? Which areas might be most important to address first?

2. Think of a specific conflict in which injustice and unequal power are important dimensions.

   a. What factors prevent individuals from taking a stand for justice?

   b. Describe how the parties are currently engaging each other. What needs to change in their behavior in order to make just and peaceful outcomes possible? How could peacebuilders assist these changes to happen?

Section Two

Introduction to Mediation

CHAPTER 3

Mediation: A Tool for Empowering Others

WHO HAS THE AUTHORITY to resolve conflicts? The answer to this question says a great deal about where the real power lies in any organization, whether it be a family, neighborhood, church, school, city, or nation.

Mediation is a tool that can empower people to solve their own conflicts and take responsibility for their own lives. However, it is important to understand what mediators do and do not do if empowerment is to happen. For example:

- Mediators do not make decisions for other people or tell them what to do.

- Mediators do not seek power over the lives of others.

- Mediators do not have answers for other people's problems.

- Mediators do not bear the responsibility if mediation fails (assuming they've done a reasonably good job of mediating).

- Mediators do not take the credit if mediation is successful (even if they have done a brilliant job of mediating).

If mediators seek to empower others, they must operate in ways compatible with this goal. For example:

- Mediators must be truly committed to serving other people. Peacebuilders not genuinely willing to work as servants to others should not waste their time and endanger other people by trying to become mediators.

- Mediators must be willing to work very hard and yet see to it that the disputing parties get credit for their hard work. After all, who is empowered if the mediators claim the credit for the success?

- Mediators must see the parties themselves as the people primarily responsible for resolving a conflict. As far as possible, mediators should solicit ideas for resolution from the parties and offer their own suggestions only as a last resort.

- Mediators must consult with the parties about the negotiation process at every step of the way. Mediators should always have ideas about what to do next, but if they are to convey a sense of ownership of the discussion process to the parties, the mediators must consult with the parties about next steps throughout discussions.

- Mediators must see their task as "working themselves out of a job." Whenever possible, mediators should transfer skills and knowledge to the parties so that the parties will be able to deal with similar situations in the future without relying on a mediator.

MEDIATION VERSUS ARBITRATION

Many people confuse mediation with arbitration. Arbitration resembles mediation in that it also involves a third party assisting people in conflict to find a solution to their problem. However, whereas mediation places the responsibility to decide on acceptable solutions in the hands of the parties, arbitration places this responsibility on the arbitrator. Arbitrators listen to both sides and then, like King Solomon, pronounce a solution they believe is wise and fair.

In dozens of workshops, we have guided participants through an opening exercise in which they are asked to role-play efforts to resolve two conflicts with the assistance of a third party. In the first conflict, the peacemaker is told to take the role of an arbitrator. In the second conflict, the peacemaker is instructed to be a mediator. People are then asked to reflect on their experience of the role-playing and state their preference: Did they prefer mediation or arbitration?

Although agreeing that there is a time and a place for arbitration, groups in North America, Europe, and urban centers in Africa and Asia consistently state a preference for mediation as a means of resolving conflicts. Generally, they share the following beliefs:

- Mediation empowers people to make decisions about their own problems.

- Mediation encourages more responsible behavior in conflict situations.

- Mediation is more likely to genuinely resolve the specific conflict since both parties have a say in the solution.

- Mediation contributes to the development of individuals and communities by reducing dependence on others.

- Mediation fosters in people a greater sense of control over their own lives.

How widely, then, is mediation used in real life? Think about your own experience. When you were six years old and got in a fight with a brother or sister, did your parents use mediation or arbitration? When you were older, as a teenager in school, if you argued with classmates, which approach did your teachers use? Today, as an adult, if a conflict arises in your place of work or in your community, which approach do you see leaders using to address the conflict?

The overwhelming majority of people in workshops say that their parents and teachers almost always used arbitration. In adult life, mediation is more commonly used, but even here, at least two-thirds say that arbitration is the means selected for resolving conflicts. In short, although most people *prefer* mediation as a solution to conflict, they are far more experienced with arbitration. Consequently, when called on to help resolve a conflict, most people respond in ways that are much closer to arbitration than to mediation.

This manual focuses on mediation. For the reasons cited by workshop participants, in most family, organizational, neighborhood, community, and political conflicts, mediation assists the possibility of transformation in ways that arbitration does not. If mediation fails, arbitration can be initiated as a useful follow-up. In most communities worldwide, there are plenty of people—elders, religious and community leaders, judges, lawyers, and others—who are well versed in the art of stepping in to impose a decision. There is no need to train people in a response that is already overused. Unfortunately, the number of people skilled in mediation is far smaller. The purpose of this manual is to help fill that critical gap.

A FOUR-STAGE APPROACH TO MEDIATION

Each culture and each community is different, and therefore mediation approaches differ from one setting to another. It would be arrogant to claim that one approach to mediation is the best. Nevertheless, to keep things simple, mediation is presented in this manual as a four-stage process, which begins after advance preparation and getting the parties to the table (see Exhibit 3.1).

EXHIBIT 3.1

The Stages of Mediation.

Stage 1: Introduction   **(Providing Safety)**
- Greet, seat, and introduce the participants.
- State goals, emphasizing that this is a voluntary process for parties to reach a mutual agreement.
- Describe the mediator's role (to help the parties talk, not to judge or give answers).
- Describe the process (each side will speak in turn; then both will agree on the basic issues and will work with these one at a time with their suggestions for resolution).
- Gain commitment to the ground rules (not interrupting, confidentiality, respect).

Stage 2: Storytelling   **(Offering Understanding)**
- Get A's perspective on the situation and the mediator's summary; identify hopes and concerns.
- Get B's perspective and the mediator's summary; identify hopes and concerns.
- Listen for issues and common ground.

Stage 3: Problem Solving   **(Building Ownership)**
- Clarify the issues.
- Identify common concerns and establish common ground.
- Work on one issue at a time (usually start with the easiest to resolve).
- Maintain control by using a list of the issues and interviewing each party in turn.
- Move away from the parties' demands and focus on each party's underlying interests.
- Generate options, inviting the parties to suggest their proposals for resolution.
- Evaluate the options together.
- Select options and plan implementation.
- *At all times,* look for opportunities to
     Point out areas of commonalty and positive intentions
     Acknowledge hurt, anger, and frustration
     Suggest that parties speak directly to one another (coaching direct dialogue)
     Affirm constructive moves and highlight progress made

Stage 4: Agreement   **(Seeking Sustainability)**
- Summarize agreements reached.
- Ensure that specifics are addressed—who, what, when, where, how.
- Be realistic, clear, and simple.
- Maintain balance in the parties' responsibilities.
- Make sure the agreement is just and contributes to the dignity of each party.
- Agree on how to handle any further problems that arise.
- Ask the parties to state their intent to support the agreement.
- Write out the agreement and have the parties sign it.

If alienation has been deep, give the parties an opportunity to speak to each other in ways that will help them let go of the past and begin to restore their relationship.

   If there is no resolution, remind the parties of their confidentiality agreement, affirm the level of understanding reached, and offer to meet again.

From *Peace Skills: A Manual for Community Mediators* by Ronald S. Kraybill with Robert A. Evans and Alice Frazer Evans. Copyright © 2001 by Jossey-Bass, San Francisco, CA.

Stage 1: *Introduction*—providing a safe place for parties to begin face-to-face discussion

Stage 2: *Storytelling*—allowing the parties to express their concerns, explain the situation as they understand it, and gain a sense of the other party's view

Stage 3: *Problem Solving*—building a sense of joint ownership of problems by helping parties identify the issues that separate them and generate, evaluate, and negotiate options for resolution

Stage 4: *Agreement*—working out the terms of a fair and sustainable agreement, including ways to deal with problems that may arise later

These four stages, along with premediation, are described in the remaining chapters of Section Two. Critical skills and tools used in all of these stages are discussed in Section Three.

A MEDIATION TOOL KIT

Just as these stages are not the only way to conduct mediation, the various approaches suggested in each stage are not directives. No "road map for mediators" exists that addresses all situations. Every conflict is different and may require different responses. Rather than a road map, mediators need a tool kit. The following chapters introduce a variety of tools that belong in such a kit. In actual mediation, the order and frequency of use varies enormously. Some tools, such as *paraphrasing* and *pointing out common concerns*, are so helpful they deserve to be used repeatedly in a single mediation session. Others are effective only in unusual circumstances. When you master the tools, you will find that you are able to draw on them in response to the unique characteristics of each conflict.

To a substantial extent, the variety of tools that mediators need fall into three categories.

1. *Problem-Oriented Activities.* Significant problems or issues separate the parties. By persistently drawing out the needs and interests that the parties bring to the table in relation to these issues, mediators can make it much easier to find solutions acceptable to both. Knowing how to expand the range of options for resolution also increases chances of agreement. These problem-solving strategies can be employed to make the discussion about resolution more efficient and effective.

2. *People-Oriented Activities.* These activities address the parties' emotional needs and their relationship to each other. It is seldom, if ever, possible to deal with conflicts by talking only about the practical issues at stake.

People bring powerful emotional agendas to any discussion of their differences, and it may be impossible to resolve the issues at stake until work has been done with emotions. Simply listening to the people involved, for example, giving them a chance to express their feelings and feel heard, meets important emotional needs and sometimes enables people to move on and begin discussing issues constructively. Other commonly used *people activities* include pointing out common ground, acknowledging the parties' good intentions, encouraging them to speak directly to each other at well-timed moments, offering conciliatory statements, using procedures that require them to listen to each other, and arranging for activities that enable them to build their relationship. Helping the parties build their relationship and explore useful approaches for handling future conflicts may at times prove to be more important than solving the immediate problem.

3. *Process-Oriented Activities.* These are activities aimed at improving the process through which people in conflict interact with each other. For example, people often communicate using misleading or confusing words; mediators can improve the communication process by seeking clarity. Suggesting a change in the sequence in which problems are negotiated can be helpful. In complex negotiations, it may be wise for mediators to suggest that the parties begin, not with the issues at stake, but with a discussion of process—that is, how they will go about their talks. Which problem will they begin with? Who needs to be involved in the talks? What ground rules would they like to suggest for the discussion? What will be said to others about what is happening?

Skill in each of these areas and the capacity to shift easily from one area to another are the hallmarks of a strong mediator. When progress is blocked in one area, often it is useful to shift the focus to a different one. However, many mediators have strong preferences for one set of skills over another. A mediator who is task-oriented may find it easy to guide parties through a discussion of the practical issues and how to solve them but be unsure how to deal with outbursts of emotion or how to enable the parties to find common ground. Another mediator may find it easy to work with the feelings of the parties but have difficulty moving from this relationship-oriented activity to guiding the parties in resolving the practical problems they face.

Learning to mediate is not a matter of memorizing a prescribed model but rather one of developing proficiency in a variety of mediation tasks and strategies. It is also a matter of learning about your own skills and abilities, where you need to improve, and when to involve a co-mediator who complements your skills.

APPLICATION EXERCISE

Think about a time when you were involved in efforts to resolve a conflict, as a party or as a peacemaker:

1. Did you begin by focusing on the people, the problem, or the process?

2. Do you find one of the three areas of focus easier than the others? Harder?

CHAPTER 4

Before Mediation: Laying the Foundation

MEDIATION CANNOT SUCCEED without the proper groundwork. Three tasks are indispensable: getting the parties to participate, selecting mediators, and preparing oneself for mediation.

GETTING THE PARTIES TO THE TABLE

The biggest challenge for peacebuilders is often not mediation itself but rather getting people to participate in the process. Perhaps someday it will be taken for granted that every neighborhood, organization, religious group, and community contains people skilled in assisting others to sort out serious differences, and people in conflict will jointly seek out assistance when trouble arises. But in the meantime, many conflicts require careful effort to bring both sides to a point of willingness to even meet and discuss their differences. Every situation is unique and must be dealt with on its own terms, with particular sensitivity to cultural differences. The following suggestions may help parties explore the possibility of mediation.

Separate Mediating from Premediating

Often it is more effective if the person who initiates discussion about the possibility of mediation assumes that someone else will handle the actual job of mediating. It is awkward to say to a party, "Would you like to use mediation?" when there is an additional expectation: "and by the way, I want to be the mediator." The person exploring possibilities for mediation should go with a simple agenda: to express concern for the persons involved, to establish communication with each side, to gather information from each, and to help think through possibilities for next steps. If the parties later request that this person also mediates, the option can be considered at that time.

Focus on Building Trust and Gathering Information

The goal is to *understand* the parties, not to "sell" mediation. To the extent that the parties feel others approaching them have preformed opinions about what they should do, they are likely to be mistrustful. You can usually build trust by expressing concern and care, by stating your desire to learn and understand, and by listening and paraphrasing. Only after you have done these things are the parties likely to trust your suggestions about mediation. Factors that can destroy trust are any hints of partiality or taking sides and offering advice, especially before you have a full understanding of the issues. Remember that the goal is not to solve the conflict at this stage. The goal is simply to build trust and gather enough information to be able to determine how to move things forward.

Provide Information About Mediation

Most people have no experience with mediation, and some react negatively because they do not understand it. Be prepared to describe mediation clearly and simply. It is important to do this without trying to push people into mediation, which is likely to cause them to pull away. You are more likely to be effective if your goal is providing information about mediation rather than promoting it. A story about how mediation was used in a similar situation is one effective way to do this. Often people need time to reflect on the information you offer, and this may call for more than one conversation.

Ask About the Future

Many people in conflict are so caught up in the heat of battle that they fail to consider the costs of the war. Thoughtful questions might help them begin to think about things they ought to consider:

- What are the costs of continuing in the current way?

- How can things get resolved?

- What will happen if things are not resolved?

Coordinate the Contacting of the Parties

Initiators should exercise care to contact all parties at about the same time. To meet with the second party a month after meeting with the first, for example, is likely to cause trouble. Often word travels quickly about efforts to begin mediation, and other parties may conclude that the mediators are not particularly interested in or concerned about their views. In almost all cases, it is wise to be open about the fact that you are or will be talking with the other parties as well.

Work at Similar Organizational Levels

In conflicts involving groups of people rather than a small number of individuals, it is preferable during the initiation stage to meet with people at similar levels in the various groups. Initiators or mediators should try to avoid, for example, meeting with the president of one organization to explore mediation and a low-level deputy in the opposing organization. Sometimes in early stages of exploration, there is little choice, of course, but to meet with whatever people are accessible, regardless of their levels. However, serious talks are unlikely until decision makers at similar organizational levels are engaged.

Be Alert to Cultural Differences

What may be an appropriate and effective approach in one cultural setting may be offensive in another. In some communities, for example, an older man, never a woman, would approach a younger man to encourage him to consider mediation. In another cultural context, a team of respected people would have the greatest possibility for success.

Assuming that the parties express openness to mediation, the following suggestions may help in exploring next steps.

Agree on Who Will Attend

People deal poorly with surprise and uncertainty in settings of conflict. Everyone should know exactly who is coming to a mediation session.

Agree on the Purpose of Any Meeting Between Parties

The more clearly people understand the purpose of the meeting before they arrive, the smaller the likelihood of further misunderstandings. Is the purpose just to get acquainted? Is it to work out the terms under which to conduct later negotiations? Is it to define the issues and analyze problems? Is it actually to begin the mediation process?

Agree on a Time Frame

People need a clear sense of how long the meeting will last and should be made aware that some mediations take more than one session.

Agree on the Venue

People need to agree on a neutral, easily accessible location that is comfortable for all parties.

Agree on a Choice of Mediators

Once parties are seriously considering meeting to discuss their differences, they will need to agree on the best person or persons to facilitate their discussion. The initiators who have successfully brought parties to this point must be careful not to assume that they are the best persons to play this role. Although the parties may request the initiator as mediator, the initiator should also be ready to suggest other possible mediators who may be acceptable to the parties. Some parties prefer someone whom they know well and trust from past experience. Others prefer a mediator who knows neither party and is therefore more "objective."

 For additional suggestions that focus specifically on premediation with parties in group or intergroup conflict, see "Working with Community Groups" at www.josseybass.com/peaceskills.

THE ROLE OF CO-MEDIATORS

Sometimes it is difficult to find any one person who is trusted as impartial and acceptable to both parties. In this case, a team of two or more co-mediators can work well so long as each party feels that the team is balanced in its totality. In a dispute between a young Hispanic man and an older African American woman, for example, a solo mediator is likely to be viewed with some skepticism by at least one of the parties. Co-mediators of different gender and ethnic or cultural identity can together represent impartiality and fairness. Co-mediators also bring different skills and abilities to the mediation table. Although many effective mediators work alone, co-mediation has many advantages as well as some challenges.

Advantages of Co-Mediation

- A balance in terms of diversity can assist parties in feeling more comfortable by having someone with whom they can identify. This is particularly important in conflicts involving race, ethnicity, or gender.

- Two heads are better than one in deciding on the best process or approach in difficult cases.

- Different styles and experiences can provide combined knowledge, skills, and insights.

- Co-mediators can take turns or divide up the work. For example, one may focus more on issues and facts while the other focuses on feelings or emotions, or one can lead and direct the process while the other monitors and ensures that important elements are not overlooked.

Challenges of Co-Mediation

- It requires teamwork in terms of preparation, coordination, timing, and cohesiveness.

- It requires understanding of each other's strengths, weaknesses, approaches, and techniques.

- It requires the ability to strategize and cue each other in order to stay on track.

When assembling a mediation team, meeting with your co-mediator before a session is critical. Here are some things you may want to discuss.

Building a Mediation Team

- Who will take the lead role in each step?

- How will tasks (opening statement, facilitating the storytelling and problem solving, writing the agreement, and so on) be divided?

- How will one step in when the other is in trouble? What signals will you use? How can you quietly pass the lead to your co-mediator?

- In terms of individual mediation style, how can you best complement each other?

- What does each of you do well? What do you not do well?

- What does each of you see as potential difficulties with the upcoming mediation, and how might you handle them?

If your signals cross, if you are uncertain about how to proceed, or if your co-mediator does something that you think is unwise, call a break and meet separately.

Do a joint evaluation at the end of the mediation to sharpen your skills and share insights about additional strengths and weaknesses.

PERSONAL PREPARATION

While preparing the parties for mediation, do not forget your own preparation for becoming an effective bridge between the parties.

Remind yourself of your own strengths and weaknesses as a mediator and those of your co-mediator.

In your thoughts, take a step back from the issues and the people involved. Search for any biases or prejudices you may hold. You need not "like" the parties equally, but be sure that you feel confident that you can actively work for the well-being of each. If not, help the parties find someone who can.

Get in touch with the spiritual and moral resources that motivate and sustain you during the mediation process. To the extent that your own ego and personal needs such as the desire to succeed, to be liked by others, or to earn recognition or power is a part of your own inner motivations, your presence will complicate the issues between the parties. Root yourself as deeply as you can in resources of the soul that sustain your focus on the needs of the parties rather than your own inner cravings. Meditation, prayer, and time to center awareness on a sense of connection to God are for many peacebuilders essential preparation for mediating.

Expect to enter the mediation process as a listener and learner. Even if you have met separately with the parties, do not assume you understand the issues or the parties' real needs and interests. They themselves are often unable to express these clearly in the beginning. Part of your task is to listen so well that you can hear things they may not have fully recognized themselves.

Remember that the long-term goals of building relationships and empowering people to address systemic injustices are sometimes more important than reaching any specific agreements.

APPLICATION EXERCISES

1. When you facilitate a discussion or help friends or family members who are in conflict, what are your most helpful attributes? What skills would you look for in a co-mediator?

2. When you are getting ready for a difficult task, what is the source of your strength? What sustains you when things are not going well? Consider your culture and family values, your religious faith, and the moral principles that guide your decisions.

3. In a role-play, practice convincing a friend to meet with someone with whom the friend is in conflict. Ask your friend what approaches were most effective. What should you avoid doing?

CHAPTER 5

The Introduction Stage: Providing Safety

THE BEGINNING of a mediation session sets the tone for the whole discussion. People usually agree to mediation because they hope that talking might improve things. When they arrive for the first session, however, the parties normally seem the opposite of hopeful. Often they are anxious and tense, suspicious of the other side, fearful of being manipulated or taken advantage of, afraid their real concerns will not be heard or understood, afraid that things will escalate out of control, and unclear about what happens in a mediation session and what to expect from the mediators.

GETTING OFF ON THE RIGHT FOOT

Getting things off on the right foot in an atmosphere of fear and mistrust is a critical first step in mediating. Consequently, the first task of mediators is to provide a safe space in which the parties feel comfortable, accepted, and respected. Mediators can do a number of things to accomplish this.

1. *Arrive at the agreed meeting place well in advance of the parties.* This gives you time to think through where people will sit, to post flipcharts, and to prepare to greet people as they arrive.

2. *Create a physical space that is comfortable and supports good interaction.* "Take charge of the space," the saying goes, "or it will take charge of you." Good facilitation begins with a critical examination of the facilities and arrangement of the space to make it best serve the purposes of the meeting. A room that is too big and full of empty space makes people just as uncomfortable as one that is too small and crowded.

The arrangement of chairs is even more important than the size of the room. In most cultures, a circle or triangle arrangement supports a more constructive atmosphere than rows, which is the arrangement mediators find upon arrival at many venues.

No arrangement is "right" for all cultures or all phases of mediation. What is important is that mediators learn to think critically about the space they are using and to take initiative in adapting it to support the purposes of the moment. The main criterion in the early stages of mediation should be a seating arrangement that makes the parties feel comfortable and safe. This usually rules out "creative" arrangements intended to encourage interaction. For example, it is not usually advisable to seat together people from opposing parties. When people come to discuss a serious conflict, they are anxious, and the first concern of mediators should be to help reduce that anxiety. If the mediation goes well, it may be effective to mix people together for interaction later in the process. But in the beginning, arrange seats to help people feel secure. Usually, that means allowing them to sit close to their own colleagues. Where should co-mediators sit? Most find that they are more effective and can better communicate with one another when they are seated together.

Plan room arrangements in advance. You will likely need a flipchart or chalkboard for jotting things down, a separate meeting room or private hallway if you expect to meet privately with the parties at any point, arrangements for smoking and toilets, and refreshments if desired. Some mediators prefer tables to make it easy to take personal notes and to give parties a sense of dignity and security. Others prefer the flexibility and sense of fewer barriers created by using chairs only.

Establish a sense of safety. Take charge from the moment the parties arrive so that there is no question that the mediators are in control. Mediators should decide in advance who will sit where and, when the parties arrive, show them where to sit. Mediators should also think through how to make introductions and how to begin the session. Later in the mediation process, if things are going well, the mediators can and should reduce their level of control, but in the beginning, it is reassuring to anxious parties to see that the mediator is clearly in charge. For them, the mediator's ability to control the situation is their only protection from chaos.

WHAT TO SAY: INTRODUCTORY COMMENTS

Many mediators find it useful to develop a standard outline of things that need to be said in the opening minutes of a mediation session, but what to say and how to say it will vary greatly with the circumstances. Mediators' opening comments often cover five important areas.

1. *Welcome and greetings.* In some cultural settings, this phase would be handled in a minute or two; in others, socializing is an important part of getting started and might take much longer.

One mediator, after welcoming the parties and showing them where to sit, looked around the small circle of tense faces before her and began a mediation session with these words: "I'd like to open by saying that I have a great deal of respect for each person gathered here for being willing to sit down and try to address differences openly. I have seen many situations like this where people simply turned their backs and refused to speak with each other. I'm sure that we have a real challenge before us today, but the mere fact that you have agreed to meet here to speak with each other makes me feel hopeful." She then went on to explain what would happen in the meeting. As she spoke, the faces of the parties began ever so slightly to lighten. By beginning on a positive and respectful note, this mediator had taken an important step toward providing safety and establishing trust between her and the parties.

2. *Names.* Sometimes social protocols are unclear, and people may be uncertain about how to address each other—by first name, surname, or title. It may be helpful to deal with this issue by indicating how you, the mediators, would like to be addressed and asking the parties to say how they would like to be addressed—for example, "My name is Ron Kraybill. Please call me Ron. What shall we call you?"

3. *Description of the next steps.* Most people have little idea about what happens in a mediation session, and therefore they benefit from a brief description. Here is one simple outline of the mediation process:

- *Each of you will be given uninterrupted time to describe the situation as you understand it.*

- *Together we will create a list of the issues of disagreement.*

- *We will discuss these issues one at a time.*

- *We will try to work out an agreement that is acceptable to all of you.*

4. *Mediators' role.* Parties often arrive expecting the mediator to be an arbitrator or a judge, determining who is right and making decisions for the parties. It therefore helps to clarify the mediators' role at the outset. The mediators might describe their role as follows. "We are not here to tell you what to do or to decide who is right or wrong. We are here to help you find *your own* solution, we look to you to decide the answers."

5. *Ground rules.* Some mediators propose ground rules; others ask the parties to suggest guidelines that will make them comfortable during the mediation. These might include not interrupting when the other party is speaking; respecting the other party, even if you don't agree with what was said; and maintaining confidentiality, if that is a concern. However, don't go overboard with ground rules; they may be perceived as demeaning to the participants, implying that these people are too uncivilized to behave appropriately unless forced to do so by rules. Usually, a few simple guidelines, such as "no interruptions" and "respect for the other party," are adequate. Ground rules are effective only if each party agrees at the beginning to abide by them. The mediators can then later remind the parties of their agreement if the ground rules are broken.

A Sample Opening Statement by Co-Mediators

The mediators meet the parties at the door, show them where to sit, and exchange appropriate greetings. Then the first mediator begins:

> The purpose of our meeting this evening is to discuss problems that have arisen between you and to try to work out a solution. We want both of you to know that we have a lot of respect for your willingness to sit down and talk things out face to face like this. First, we want to explain how we will proceed, so you know what will be happening. We will begin by asking each of you to describe the situation as you understand it. This will be a time for each of you to explain to us as mediators, without interruption from one another, exactly how you view things. We will do our best to understand how it looks from your side. After we've heard from both of you, we will try to make a list of the issues of disagreement. Then we will work with you in examining exactly what each of you needs to solve this situation and what your ideas for resolution are. The goal is to find a solution that both of you can accept.

By prearrangement, the second mediator picks up at this point:

> We would like you to understand our role here. We think it is important for you to sort out your own solutions to your problems. You are the ones involved, so we want you to decide what the solution will be. We will not be judges, saying who is right or wrong or telling you what you must do.
>
> Last of all, there is one ground rule that we would like to ask each of you to agree to: not to interrupt when the other person is speaking. This is especially important in the next part of our discussion.
>
> Mr. East, can you agree to observe this ground rule? *(Waits for a response)*
>
> Mr. West, can you agree to observe this rule? *(Waits for a response)*

The first mediator takes the lead again, moving to the Storytelling Stage:

> We'd like to begin now by inviting each of you to explain the situation as you see it. Mr. East, will you begin? Mr. West, we will ask you to listen along with us now as Mr. East speaks. In a few minutes, it will be your turn. Mr. East, you can go ahead and begin now.

PROVIDING A SAFE PLACE

Mediation is at one level a technical process calling for skills in planning meetings and agendas, information sharing, problem solving, and negotiation. At a deeper level, mediation is also a moral and spiritual process. Technical skills are useful, but they accomplish nothing if the process is not compassionately and carefully facilitated.

The foundation of the deeper process is *safety.* Breakthroughs of any kind are unlikely unless the parties feel that they are in a *safe place*. Physical safety is obviously part of being in a safe place. But other kinds of safety are equally important to the mediation process. Parties need to see the mediators do and say things that assure them on the following points:

- The mediators will treat them with respect at all times. So long as the mediators offer them a sustaining level of care, respect, and appreciation, the parties can usually cope with a substantial lack of respect from each other.

- They will not be left defenseless in the face of verbal attacks. What people think is a verbal attack varies. But parties who believe that they have been unfairly attacked and not given proper protection or means to respond will often withdraw emotionally from the discussion or retaliate by becoming aggressive.

- The mediators are personally secure, "know what they are doing," and are strong enough to maintain order and fairness.

The Introduction Stage is about far more than getting things started. More than anything else, it is about creating a safe space. Clear, well-prepared, confident, and impartial leadership by the mediators in the early minutes of the session establishes this space and opens the door to it. For now, the space is small, and there is no guarantee the parties will choose to enter it. But in the exchanges to come, the parties will have the opportunity to enter and expand it if they choose.

APPLICATION EXERCISES

1. Practice using your own words and phrases to introduce a mediation session. You may want to begin by writing down the essential components or even what you want to say, but practice until you feel comfortable without referring to your notes.

2. Consider what special room or site arrangements may be important for helping people of your own cultural background feel comfortable and safe.

CHAPTER 6

The Storytelling Stage: Offering Understanding

IF CONFLICT TRANSFORMATION begins in a place of safety, it continues in the presence of *understanding*. Transformation seeks more than mere agreement: it seeks to connect with the hearts of the individuals involved in conflict, enabling them to look at themselves and each other in a new way. There is little chance of this happening unless the parties trust that those involved in the mediation process understand them, their aspirations, and their struggles. Thus to relate to each party in ways that say "I understand" or "I am trying hard to understand you" is an essential contribution that mediators can make toward establishing a transformative conversation. This does not mean that the mediators actively try to get the parties to understand *each other* in early stages of mediation. That usually becomes possible only later in the mediation process. Understanding in mediation begins with a much more modest goal: for the parties to know that they are understood *by the mediators.* The Storytelling Stage accomplishes this critical task, particularly if mediators are good at the listening skills described in Chapter Eleven.

Three basic activities take place in this stage.

- The parties each tell their story without interruption.

- Using their own words, the mediators summarize each speaker's story.

- The mediators listen analytically to the stories in order to identify the central issues in the conflict and the concerns that the parties have in common.

WHO GOES FIRST?

Mediators use a variety of ways to determine which party speaks first. One way is to begin with the party who initiated the complaint or made the request for mediation. Another is to begin with the party who seems most in need of "venting" feelings. After letting off steam, this person may be able to listen better when it is the other party's turn to speak. Be sensitive to perceptions of equality or inequality. If a woman is mediating between a man and a woman, for example, she might ask the man to speak first. If one party feels more vulnerable or weaker, beginning first may be empowering. Ask the party not selected if your choice is acceptable. If necessary, flip a coin.

UNDERSTANDING AS THE PRIMARY GOAL

Earning the trust of the parties is more important for the mediator at this stage than mastering all the facts of the situation. Grasping facts and the sequence of what happened is obviously useful, but if you make this your primary goal, you are likely to end up interrupting the parties with constant questions and creating an atmosphere of interrogation. Allow speakers to finish their accounts and only then raise questions, or hold most of your questions until the Problem-Solving Stage, which follows. In any case, you will be more effective in earning trust if you learn ways of interacting with the parties that do not require you to rely heavily on traditional methods of asking questions.

QUESTIONS AND STATEMENTS

The question is one of the most frequently abused forms of communication. Many conflicts are actually conducted in the form of questions. Consider an argument between a husband who has arrived home late from work and his wife who greets him at the door:

Wife: "Who do you think you are, coming home at this hour?"

Husband: "Who do *you* think I am? Do you think I enjoy coming home late any more than you do?"

Wife: "How am I supposed to keep a family going if you get home late and the children are screaming the whole time? Why don't you ever let me know you're going to be late?"

Husband: "How can I call when I'm out on a job site with no telephones?"

This husband and wife have frustrations they need to express. However, rather than stating those feelings openly and really listening to each other, they are attacking with accusations dressed up as questions. They would probably come to an understanding more easily if each described his or her own feelings with statements and listened carefully as the other person did the same.

Wife: "I'm so glad you're home. It's frustrating for me when you're late. I worry that something might have happened to you. The children get tired waiting to eat, and all of us get really grouchy! I don't like it at all!"

Husband: "Sounds like you've had a rough time of it. It's been hard for me too. The last load of cement arrived late, and we had to stay to pour it. I know you like to know if I'm going to be late, but there were no telephones around. I'm tired and hungry and pretty frustrated myself."

A professor gave a communications class an assignment to get through the next twenty-four hours without asking any questions. If the students needed something, they had to find a way to get information or assistance by making a statement rather than by asking a question. They discovered that in many situations where they normally would have asked a question, a statement was actually clearer and more effective.

Questions are especially problematic where trust is low. Questions often subtly control the persons being questioned, limiting the ways in which they can respond. For this reason, questions are frequently used by lawyers in a courtroom or by police in interrogating suspects. For example, "Did you or did you not . . . ?" or "What were you doing on the evening of March 19?" Behind the question in such settings lies a hidden agenda—to trap the speaker. Where trust is low, questions tend to arouse defensiveness and resentment. Even where trust is high, communication is likely to become clearer and more effective if people use questions only when questions are truly needed.

One alternative to questions is to use statements that invite people to share information. Instead of asking, "Who is Mrs. South?" "What did you do then?" or "Why did you do that?" try saying, "Please say more about Mrs. South," "Fill us in on what you did next," or "Tell us what happened that day." Rather than using interrogatives—*who, why, what, when, how*—use gentler imperatives, statements that urge the parties to *describe, clarify,* or *say more about.* Statements do the job just as well and can create a greater sense of openness at the same time.

Questions can, of course, be used sincerely, without intending to trap or interrogate others. The right kind of question can have an important positive role if used skillfully. An open question ("What are you most concerned about?") can be used to invite a person to provide additional information. Closed questions that call for a specific answer ("What time did you get home?") seldom build trust. When people are confident that they will be heard and understood, they are more willing to share their primary concerns. (Additional suggestions of nonthreatening approaches to discover the parties' real needs and interests, which are often hidden beneath their initial demands or declared positions, are given in Chapter Seven, "Focus on Interests.")

DEALING WITH INTERRUPTIONS

A major challenge, particularly in the early stages of mediation, is dealing with interruptions from the parties. Both sides are so eager to be listened to and so fearful that they will not be understood that they often repeatedly interrupt each other. It is important that mediators develop good skills to monitor and manage this. This does not mean that mediators must at every moment in all settings insist on "one at a time." Some cultures and some individuals take freewheeling exchanges and interruptions for granted. Rigidity on the part of mediators about "taking turns" will make mediation seem artificial to such participants. But interruptions can quickly escalate into a shouting match or, more subtly, block each side from ever going deeply enough into its story to surface the underlying hurts, fragile hopes, and tentative ideas that often lead to transformation. Thus mediators should master the ability to block interruptions and maintain maximum control. Equipped with these skills, they can monitor the dynamics of each conversation carefully and determine moment by moment whether to tighten or relax their control over interaction between the parties.

Perhaps the most common strategy in reducing interruptions is to be prompt and firm in enforcing the ground rule of "no interruptions." Respond immediately to the first few interruptions and selectively ignore those that come later, not the other way around. Have pen and paper handy, and give these to the interrupter to make notes—for example, "Excuse me, Mr. North. I'd like to remind you of our ground rule about not interrupting. Here's a pen and paper. Maybe you could make notes of your concerns so you don't forget them. We'll give you a chance to respond later. Thank you. Continue now, please, Mrs. South." Another approach that slows interruptions and promotes better listening is to give the parties paper and pen at the outset and ask them to jot down any new information they hear while the other party is speaking.

A different approach, borrowed from the Native traditions of North America, is to use a "talking stick." The ground rule is that no one can speak unless he or she is holding the "talking stick" (or whatever other object is chosen). If tension is high, have each party after speaking return the object to the mediator, who then passes it to the next speaker. After the parties have had a chance to see how mediation works, they realize that everyone will be heard, and interruptions usually become much less of a problem.

DEALING WITH PROVOCATIVE STATEMENTS

Often in the Storytelling Stage, people say things that are highly provocative. "Our housing forum was going fine until those bandits sitting across the table decided we were easy prey." Mediators can respond in several ways:

- If you sense that someone is getting provoked by the account of an opponent, you can say: "John, I know you have a different perspective. I want to hear your view as well in a few minutes." Offered as an occasional aside to listening parties, such a comment by the mediator can help keep anger under control.

- Soften or "launder" provocative comments with a neutral paraphrase. For example, paraphrase "she's lying" into "you see things differently than she does." (See Chapter Twelve for further discussion of this skill.)

- Ask for specific examples. If East says West is "inconsiderate and totally irresponsible," respond by saying: "Please give us a specific example of what you have in mind." Specific examples move the discussion out of the category of character assassination and into the arena of specifics, where there is often more room for negotiation or "agreeing to disagree." (For additional suggestions, see the discussion of generalities in Chapter Twelve.)

- If name-calling or swearing becomes a prominent feature of the discussion, reiterate the ground rule of "respect" or propose a specific guideline to fit the situation. Get the commitment of both parties to observe this ground rule.

- If an emotional explosion takes place, and the mediators feel they have no other means of regaining control, they can ask to "caucus" or meet separately with each of the parties. Shuttling back and forth between the parties in separate sessions gives the mediators maximum control over the atmosphere. (The use of caucus is described further in Chapter Eight.)

How Mediators Control Interruptions

The mediators have completed their opening comments, and the parties have agreed to the ground rule of not interrupting each other. Justo, one of the mediators, now moves things into the Storytelling Stage by saying, "Let's begin our discussion by giving each of you a chance to explain what has brought you here today. Aretha, as you were the one who first requested this meeting, perhaps we will begin with you. Rosa, I'd like to remind you that this is a time to listen without interruptions. I'm sure your views will be different from Aretha's, and when we come to you, you can explain how you see things." Rosa nods. Justo continues, "Aretha, begin wherever you'd like, to help us understand your view of what is happening."

Aretha immediately turns to Rosa and says, "Rosa, you know as well as I do that you are the one who started all this." Justo is alert and recognizes that allowing the parties to address each other directly at this early and volatile stage of the discussion will bring trouble. He quickly stops Aretha: "Excuse me, Aretha. For the moment, I'd like to ask you to address your comments to us as mediators. Later there will be opportunity for you and Rosa to speak directly to each other." Aretha sighs and begins speaking to Justo.

"Well, like I was saying, Rosa is the one who started all this. On the day that our family moved into the community, . . ." Aretha goes into a long account of the troubles Rosa has caused her family as the mediators listen attentively. At one point, Rosa reacts angrily to Aretha's words and tries to break in. Justo holds up his hand and stops her. "Excuse me, Rosa. I know that you have a different understanding of this, and we'll be coming to you soon to hear your side of it. I want to remind you of the ground rule about not interrupting." Rosa is upset and begins to argue with Justo. Lynn, who is

co-mediating with Justo, assures Rosa that her turn will come soon and asks her to hold her comments until then. Rosa turns her body away and withdraws into fidgety silence, gazing at the ceiling and floor as Aretha continues.

After Aretha has been speaking for nearly fifteen minutes, Lynn breaks in gently. "Aretha, we need to give Rosa a chance to speak before long. Could you try to wrap things up soon? Give us just the key events that we need to know." Aretha continues for several more minutes and finally ends. Justo addresses Aretha, summarizing in a few sentences the events Aretha has been recounting for the past twenty minutes. "Aretha, before we hear from Rosa, I'd like to make sure that we understand the key events here as you have described them. You're saying this began ten years ago on the day you moved into the community. You were angry and hurt by things Rosa said to you about being strangers. There were several incidents after that between the children when you felt that Rosa influenced her children to act aggressively toward your children. Two weeks ago, a window was broken when the children were playing, and you want Rosa to pay for the repair costs. Two major frustrations for you throughout all of this have been that music is played late at night and that you feel Rosa talks about you to other people. Aretha, do you feel that I'm accurately understanding your side of things?" Aretha nods.

Justo now turns to Rosa. "Rosa, let's hear from you now. I just want to remind you, Aretha, that now it's your turn to listen without interruption." Aretha nods, and Rosa offers her account, a story so different from Aretha's that to the mediators it sounds almost like a different situation. When she is finished, Justo summarizes her accounts and asks if she feels he has understood her.

TAKING NOTES AND LISTENING FOR ISSUES

Along with building trust through careful listening and using statements of inquiry to draw out information about the conflict situation, mediators also listen carefully and note the central issues that must be addressed to resolve the conflict. Keeping track of all that is said presents a major challenge. It is tempting for mediators to take detailed notes, but this can be a block to building trust. A mediator whose nose is stuck in a writing pad does not convey deep personal interest in the parties! The parties need support and human contact if they are to open themselves to new and unfamiliar ways of communicating. Listening and jotting down only key words or phrases keeps writing to a minimum. If there are two mediators, another option is to agree that only one mediator at a time will take notes. This ensures that at least one person is always giving full attention to the parties. If any participants are concerned about confidentiality, ask permission before taking notes. Explain that notes will aid you during the conversation, and that you will commit to destroy them at the end of the session.

BUILDING ON SAFETY AND UNDERSTANDING

The Introduction Stage focuses on providing safety; Storytelling highlights offering understanding. These are important, practical components of the mediation process. However, mediators as peacebuilders can also draw on the moral and spiritual resources that enable them to go beyond using techniques to expressing genuine caring, concern, and acceptance of parties and communities caught in the pain and confusion of difficult conflicts. A vision of peaceful and just communities can motivate and sustain peacebuilders to move beyond "getting an agreement" to focus on an even more important goal: building or restoring relationships of honesty and respect among those in conflict.

APPLICATION EXERCISES

1. One of the best ways to practice summarizing is to share stories with a partner. One person shares a personal story of a specific event or series of events for about five minutes. The listener then offers a brief summary. When the listener is finished, the storyteller evaluates the extent to which the listener has captured the central dimensions of the story. Then exchange roles and repeat the exercise.

2. The example of storytelling in the sidebar "How Mediators Control Interruptions" illustrates a high level of mediator intervention. Would this approach be appropriate in mediating among your friends and colleagues? If not, in what ways would you relax it? Talk with another person in your own community about how much room mediators should allow for parties to interrupt each other during mediation.

3. In preparation for the Problem-Solving Stage, reread Justo's summary of Aretha's account in the sidebar. What key words or phrases describe the issues for Aretha? Look for unbiased ways to describe these issues. The mediator will be developing a similar set of key words or phrases for Rosa's issues. This list is an important tool in the next stage.

CHAPTER 7

The Problem-Solving Stage: Building Joint Ownership

THE PROBLEM-SOLVING STAGE usually marks the beginning of the most challenging part of mediation. The telling of conflicting stories may be difficult enough, but things often get trickier as parties think about whether and how to weave those stories together in the future. Many mediators begin to feel a strong inner push in this stage, a desire to be "successful" in their role and to see the parties at peace. This desire often forces mediators out of a facilitative role and into arbitration. Rather than keeping the burden of responsibility on the parties to develop their own solutions to the problems they share, mediators may begin to shoulder this responsibility themselves. They may increasingly shift from a focus on assisting the parties to talk with each other to trying to convince the parties to accept solutions advocated by the mediators.

The goal of transformation requires mediators to resist this dynamic and instead work in ways that build a sense of joint ownership among parties for solving their problems themselves. How this is done will differ according to the nature of the problem, the number of people, and the different cultures involved. In cultures that place a high value on harmony and relationships, parties may expect to engage in lengthy, cautious exchanges to establish a human connection between them before attempting problem solving, and even then, problem solving may be indirect. By contrast, in cultures that value efficiency and concrete results, the parties are likely to expect to move rapidly into open problem solving. However, for learning mediation, it is useful to have in mind a sample sequence of activities to guide the steps after the Storytelling Stage.

During storytelling, mediators listen carefully to the stories and begin to identify the central issues in the conflict and what the parties have in common. In problem solving they might continue as follows:

1. *Clarify the issues.* Summarize in a list the issues that appear to need to be addressed to resolve the conflict.

2. *Identify common concerns.* Point out what the parties share in common to build a cooperative climate for discussing what divides them.

3. *Select one issue.* Provide focus to keep the parties from wandering from one topic to another.

4. *Focus on interests.* Return to storytelling to clarify the selected issue and draw out the parties in ways that move them away from their demands to draw forth their underlying interests.

5. *Generate options.* To improve the possibility of finding mutually acceptable agreements, help the parties develop a range of ideas for resolution.

6. *Evaluate and choose options.* Guide the parties in analyzing the strengths and weaknesses of the various options, and select those that best meet their interests.

We shall discuss each of these steps in turn.

CLARIFY THE ISSUES

This step requires knowing how to recognize the problems or issues that separate people, how to describe them impartially, and how to summarize or list them visually.

Return to the list of issues you developed in Chapter Six, Application Exercise 3, and see how your list compares to the list used by the mediators in the neighborhood conflict between Aretha and Rosa. The parties have just finished storytelling, and one mediator clarifies the issues as the first step in the Problem-Solving Stage:

> Thanks to both of you for your accounts. Before moving on, I want to try to summarize the issues that seem to be coming out of the discussion so far. One issue seems to be the children. Both of you have talked about your frustration with the children of the other family. Another is the window that got broken last week. Also, there seems to be a problem about music in the evening. In addition, both of you have felt the other person has been spreading rumors about you, so it may be useful to talk about more constructive ways of dealing with conflicts between you in the future. Do you feel that this list covers the things we need to talk about?

This step advances the process in several ways. First of all, the parties are often confused about what the conflict is actually about or disagree about the causes. They also typically think that the divisions separating them are bigger or more numerous than they actually are. "I was surprised when you summarized the issues between us," a party once commented near the end of a mediation session. "Before we started, it seemed like there were a lot more than three issues." Clarifying the issues can make the conflict seem more manageable.

Furthermore, it is difficult to maintain control of the discussion if the parties have not agreed on the issues for discussion. Having a visible "agenda" is one of the mediator's most powerful tools in establishing an atmosphere of impartiality and maintaining control over the discussion process.

List the Issues

In some situations, the mediator's verbal summary of the issues is sufficient. However, listing the issues on a flipchart or chalkboard at the beginning of the Problem-Solving Stage can provide a visual focus and a common reference point for the discussion. If the mediation is going well, the list gradually becomes accepted as a joint challenge, which the parties address together. Even when things are tense and hostile, a list is valuable to the mediator in maintaining control. When one party makes accusations, the mediator can say, "Let's put that on the list of issues so we don't lose it. For now, let's stick with the issue we're currently discussing."

Usually, it is best to make one list that covers the concerns of both parties. In the conflict between Aretha and Rosa, the mediator wrote the following list on a chalkboard as she was making her verbal summary.

Issues for Discussion

- Window
- Music
- Children
- Dealing with problems in the future

It is easier to develop this list if you first take notes on your own private writing pad during the Storytelling Stage. Then, as you move into problem solving, check with the parties to make sure your list reflects the things they need to talk about, and then write the list on flipchart or board.

Creating one list reinforces the awareness that the parties face joint problems that require joint efforts to solve. But sometimes the parties cannot agree on one common list of issues. In this case, you may need to create two lists, one for each party.

Even if you are working with people who are not comfortable with the written page, you can use a flipchart or chalkboard to good effect, using symbols rather than words. For mediation situations in which the parties may feel intimidated by writing, one community mediator suggests carrying a handbag or briefcase containing a variety of small objects. Instead of writing a list of issues on a flipchart, simply pull items from the bag and set them on the table to represent the issues under discussion!

A flipchart or chalkboard can be used for things other than listing issues. You might also use it to list common concerns, to record a variety of options for resolving an issue, to assess the strengths and weaknesses of particular options under consideration, or to summarize points of agreement that emerge. If the mediation continues over several sessions, and the parties agree, you can keep the flipchart and use it at the beginning of later sessions to review progress. This visual medium is a valuable tool in breaking down the walls of division.

Choose Impartial Words

In describing issues, it is important to choose words carefully so as not to imply partiality or judgment. It would only make the conflict worse, for example, if the mediator were to list the Aretha-Rosa issues like this:

- Window broken by Rosa's son

- Rosa's irresponsible partying and loud radio

- Rudeness of Aretha's children

Listing the issues in this way would make each party feel that the mediator agreed with the other side, and the atmosphere would probably immediately turn defensive and hostile. Participants are very sensitive to the way mediators talk about their problems and issues. The wrong choice of words can reduce a party's trust in the mediators or provoke arguments with them. Mediators should therefore be careful to choose neutral words that identify issues without allocating blame.

IDENTIFY COMMON CONCERNS

Think of a time when you have been angry with someone you care about. In the midst of that conflict, were you aware of how much you cared about that person or of the things you shared in common? Probably not. People in conflict get so caught up in the heat of disagreement that they often lose perspective of the total picture. This makes the damage of conflict much greater than it needs to be. Even when people may not care for each other personally, they often agree on important things, share certain values or goals, or need each other. Mediators can become a moderating force by repeatedly reminding participants of things they agree on or have in common. This helps the parties make decisions based on more than the anger and resentment they feel at the moment.

One good time to summarize points of agreement is after the parties have agreed on the list of issues needing discussion and before they have actually begun in-depth discussion. It is possible in almost any conflict situation to find points that the parties have in common:

- They are both likely to benefit from resolution of the conflict.

- The fact that they are willing to attend the mediation session indicates a desire to resolve things.

- Both parties may have said that this conflict has been painful, frustrating, costly, or burdensome.

- The parties may have each made statements indicating high commitment to the same institution, religious community, neighborhood, or family.

- The parties may have talked about steps they took in the past to try to resolve things. Even if these failed, the efforts indicate an intention to work things out.

- They may be victims of the same larger social forces, such as unemployment, racial discrimination, violence, or low wages.

- They may have indicated that they have made mistakes or overreacted in the past.

It is usually possible to recognize several areas that the parties agree on or have in common, even in the most polarized conflict. Pointing these out repeatedly throughout the discussion process can improve the emotional atmosphere of discussion. But be cautious! There are also a number of things you should not do when pointing out commonalties:

- Do *not* make up nice things that are not true. Be sure that any commonalties you talk about reflect things the parties have already said or facts that are obviously true.

- Do *not* tell the parties that they do not have any real disagreements or that their disagreements are not significant. At all times, the mediator accepts that the conflicts are serious and real. In highlighting common concerns, you are merely pointing out that in addition to the areas of conflict, there are also some areas where the parties agree.

• Do *not* suggest that resolution is going to be easy. On the contrary, the point is that there is hard work ahead, and as the parties begin this work, it is helpful for them to remember what they have in common.

Your credibility as a mediator is probably your most important asset with the parties. Never lie and never exaggerate the prospects for agreement or peace. Whatever commonalties you point out have to be real and believable.

SELECT ONE ISSUE

After the issues have been identified, mediators face a strategic choice: With which issue to begin? There are various ways to make this decision:

• *Order of importance.* Pick the one or two most important issues. When completed, continue with the next most important. This approach is effective when the atmosphere is good but difficult when tension is high. Parties may disagree about which issues are most important. Then too, anxious or angry parties often need some successes in less significant areas before they can begin thinking about cooperation in more important areas.

• *Easiest first.* This is the opposite tack, useful when things are tense. This approach is probably more widely used than any other because success with small items creates momentum for larger ones that follow.

• *Long-term versus short-term.* Separate the problems into two lists, long-term and short-term. Then begin with whichever list seems easier to resolve—usually the list of short-term problems.

• *Alternating choice.* Parties take turns to pick issues for discussion.

• *Principles first, then specifics.* Begin by negotiating criteria any potential agreement must meet. For example, two organizations were in conflict over similar services that both sought to provide to a local community. In talks to end the squabbling, the directors began problem solving by negotiating the following criteria for any agreement:

> We agree that the ideal solution would (a) enable both organizations to continue working in the community without destructive competition, (b) not require any job loss in either organization, and (c) enable us to coordinate our community service activities wherever possible.

They then proceeded to work out an agreement that specified how to implement these guiding principles. This strategy is particularly effective in conflicts that are complex or that involve large numbers of people.

• *Building blocks.* Issues are dealt with in a logical sequence by determining which issues lay groundwork for decisions about later ones. For example, "We'll begin with the issue of job description since the issue of salary level depends on the job description."

Regardless of how the decision is made, no one party should be allowed to decide which issue to begin with, as this may create the impression that the mediators have given control of the discussion process to one side. The decision should be made by the mediators or jointly by the parties.

FOCUS ON INTERESTS

Deepen the Level of Discussion

Once a specific issue has been selected for discussion, the mediator can return the discussion to a form of storytelling:

> I'd like you to take turns again, just like we did when we began our meeting and I asked you to share what you were most concerned about. I suggest that we discuss the issue of the window first. Aretha, perhaps you could tell me about what happened with the window from your perspective, and then Rosa, I'd like to hear your perspective on the incident as well.

The discussion begins well, but the parties soon wander off the topic and begin making accusations.

Aretha: *(speaking to the mediator about Rosa)* I want to know when she's going to pay me for my window that her child broke. It cost me forty dollars to replace!

Rosa: You have no proof my son broke that window! It might have been some other child! Anyway, you deserve a broken window for the way your children pick on my boy. If you'd get your children to act civilized, the whole neighborhood wouldn't be upset at you!

Aretha: Civilized! You're telling me about being civilized? You're the one who plays trashy music until midnight, so loud nobody else can sleep! That's how this whole thing got started!

When a discussion bounces rapidly from one issue to another, it is unlikely that the parties will be able to move to the deeper levels of awareness essential to transformation. A mediator can help the parties go deeper in several ways.

Focus on the Issues—Again

One helpful mediator response may be to remind the parties of the ground rule not to interrupt. Another approach would be to refocus the discussion, directing attention to a single issue, preferably an easy one:

> Let me just say something here. We agreed that you need to talk about the children—as you can see, we have this issue here on the list, but we can only talk about one thing at a time. I'd like to suggest that we continue discussing the question of the window and set aside matters about the children until we've heard from each of you about what happened with the window.

The mediator used the posted list of issues to stop an unhelpful exchange and to focus on a single issue. The reason for doing this is not that the issues are the only things worth talking about. For example, strong feelings are present and may need expression and discussion as well. But returning the discussion to the issues constructively directs attention toward solving a problem rather than defeating an opponent. Further steps are needed, as follows.

Move from Demands to Interests

The factual details of the window incident have already been given by the parties, but they soon begin to repeat their demands:

Aretha: *(speaking to the mediator about Rosa)* She still has to pay me for the window her children broke. She owes me forty bucks!

Rosa: I'm not about to pay you anything. You've got no proof it was my boy!

Many mediations quickly come to this point, with the parties each taking rigid positions. Unless something changes the dynamics, this kind of discussion can go on for a long time with no resolution. The parties state and restate their demands, getting a little louder with each round, and in the end the talks accomplish nothing. How can a mediator move the conversation beyond the mere stating of angry demands to a more constructive level?

It helps to recognize that a demand is in fact a solution to a deeper problem. In the example, Aretha sees payment for the window as the only solution. What is the deeper, underlying problem or concern that motivates her demand? If the discussion moves in this direction, it often becomes apparent that there may be other solutions to the conflict, and the atmosphere improves.

Another way of saying this: recognize the difference between *demands* and *interests.* Parties in conflict take positions and make *demands* about what the other party must do to resolve the conflict. They often battle intensely over these demands, assuming that looking after themselves requires strengthening their own position and attacking their opponent's. But behind the demands lie *interests,* the deeper needs or concerns that are ultimately more important to the parties. It is here that the real possibilities for resolution lie.

"Ignore demands and focus on the underlying interests" is a strategy that assists in many situations.[1] Criticizing people or their demands or trying to get parties to compromise and "back off" from their demands only causes them to cling more stubbornly to them. Rather than challenging the demands that people put forward, quietly move the discussion to the underlying interest or need. This begins by seeking more information, using open questions to draw out the parties.

Mediator: Rosa, you seem confident your son wasn't involved in the window breaking. Could you say a bit more about this?

Rosa: Like I said, she has no proof that my son broke her window. It's only the word of her children, and they blame my son for everything that happens in the neighborhood. That's what really bugs me. I'm not saying my son is perfect, but her two gang up on my boy all the time. They intentionally do things to provoke him. She always sides with them and refuses to even listen about the stuff they're doing to my boy. The issue isn't forty bucks for a window; it's whether she's willing to face up to the fact that her kids aren't angels either!

Mediator: So for you the most important thing is being able to sort out what's happening between the children. *(Rosa nods.)* Aretha, help me understand the reasons why you feel so strongly about payment for the window.

Aretha: Look, it didn't cost me that much to put in a new piece of glass. But that's not the point. What I'm really angry about is that child's attitude. He says the rudest things to the other children, even to adults! He thinks he can get away with anything he wants!

Mediator: So it sounds like it's not so much the cost of the glass that's important to you. What you're upset about is the things happening between her son and your children, and you feel he says and does what he wants.

The key to success in this exchange is the mediator's attitude. Instead of quickly accepting the demands as stated, the mediator takes the role of a friendly but somewhat uninformed interviewer. Her queries show she is eager to learn more about each side's perspective. She paraphrases the comments in each speaker's response in a way that emphasizes the underlying interests. This sets the stage for her to continue as follows:

Mediator: Rosa and Aretha, from your comments, it sounds like there is agreement that the cost of repairing the broken window is not really what's at stake here. Both of you are unhappy about the way the children are relating to one another. Shall we talk about this? Let's give each of you a chance to describe what you have seen happening and then see if there may be ways to address this problem.

The parties readily accepted this invitation. The discussion about the children began intensely and lasted another hour. The parents worked out a set of ground rules for play, and each agreed to "lay down the law" to her own youngsters. Having accomplished this, it took no more than two minutes to split the cost of the window repair.

Many conflicts that seem to involve direct competition between the parties prove to be more resolvable than first appearances suggest. Usually, individuals and groups are motivated not by one simple interest but by several interests. Often the parties need extensive conversation to determine whether there are sufficient interests in common to make a mediated settlement possible. The most effective approach on the part of the mediator is to be interested, concerned, and eager to understand but not to seek to impose ideas or solutions.

Sometimes parties are unwilling to reveal their real interests in the presence of opponents, and private sessions may be required to explore the interests behind their demands. But often the parties are willing to speak about their interests openly, and mediation can proceed smoothly in joint session.

Identifying interests does not solve a conflict. It is still necessary to develop solutions that address the interests that emerge. However, interests are usually less controversial than the demands people make or the positions they take. By focusing on interests, a variety of possible solutions may suddenly become apparent, even in situations that previously appeared irresolvable.

Listen for Points of Agreement

An important mediator skill is the ability to hear and build on points of agreement that emerge. As the parties discuss the issues, they often hint at ways to solve their problems. However, because larger issues are still unresolved, the tone of the discussion remains hostile. Mediators must be alert for agreements or concessions, no matter how small, and summarize these as a way of improving the atmosphere. For example, two organizations providing similar services to a community had been experiencing conflict among their staff members in the field. In a mediation session, members of each organization made a number of strong accusations, including the charge that the other was spreading rumors in the community. Then the following exchange took place:

Director of Organization A: The only way we're going to prevent this kind of thing from taking place is if fieldworkers in the two organizations meet on a regular basis and try to coordinate their activities.

Director of Organization B: Well, I agree that lack of communication among our fieldworkers has been a problem from the very beginning. But as I was saying earlier, unless there's a shift in attitude on the part of your management, we'll never solve this problem.

Mediator: It seems that both organizations came to this meeting today because you want to try to solve this problem. From what you have both just said, it sounds like you agree that it would be a good idea to establish a regular forum for fieldworkers from the two organizations to meet and coordinate their work. What would it take to make something like that successful?

Had the mediator not noted this point, a significant area of consensus would probably have passed unnoticed, since the director of Organization B had shifted the discussion back to previous criticisms he had made about Organization A. Fortunately, the mediator was alert to the point of agreement and used it well. Ten minutes later, after the directors had finished working out the details for a monthly meeting of fieldworkers from both organizations, the atmosphere was improving. It was then easier to begin discussion of more complicated issues separating the organizations.

If there is progress in mediation, the list of agreements gets longer and longer. By reminding the parties of what they have accomplished and what they have in common, the mediator reduces the chances that they will fall back into attacks and recriminations. The list of agreements already reached helps establish an atmosphere of progress and cooperation that assists in addressing more difficult issues. (For more on this, see "Hearing Hidden Offers" in Chapter Twelve.)

GENERATE OPTIONS

The more options available for consideration in resolving a conflict, the greater the chances of finding solutions that meet everyone's interests. In most conflicts, however, the number of options equals the number of parties. If there are two parties, only two options for resolution are under consideration, one from each party, and discussion consists of tense haggling over these demands.

Mediators can contribute to the resolution of a conflict by encouraging the parties to increase the number of possible options. Consider the following exchange:

Civic Leader: The only answer to this problem is for the state to build low-income housing!

Local Legislator: You know we don't have money for that. Everybody wants freebies! The initiative has to come from the community and the private sector!

Chair of Regional Housing Committee: Yes, but they can't do it themselves! We're going to have to put together a coalition that has support from the state and business, or we'll never get anywhere!

The pattern in this conversation is an unhelpful cycle of generate, evaluate, generate, evaluate. Each speaker proposes an idea that the next speaker reacts to and evaluates negatively. Sometimes this pattern works. But more often it leads to arguments and hurt feelings. Usually, it is more effective to separate the activities of generating from evaluating. A mediator might say:

> In order to organize our discussion effectively, let's first develop a list of ideas that deserve consideration in addressing the housing problems, which we all agree are so critical for our region. Not all of these ideas may be acceptable to everyone. At this point, I simply want to list ideas as people call them out and not debate them. Please hold your comments until we have finished listing them.

The parties then begin suggesting ideas, which the mediator records on a flipchart.

Methods for generating options include the following:

- *Brainstorming.* The mediator issues a call for ideas, requesting that there be no discussion during this time; nothing but ideas should be called out and listed. Brainstorming works best when it is conducted for a limited time (say, three to ten minutes) and when participants are encouraged to offer as many ideas as possible. Brainstorming should be used in situations where the parties have indicated a strong desire to resolve things. When resentment is high, parties are unlikely to be willing to participate.

- *Written suggestions.* Participants list possible solutions on cards or notepaper. The mediator then compiles a written list of these in front of the group or collects the cards and posts them.

- *Experience of others.* List solutions to similar problems that have been used elsewhere.

- *A respected outsider.* Ask a wise community leader, a respected colleague, a banker, or a religious leader to cite solutions from similar situations.

- *Caucus.* Often the parties are more open to creative thinking in private caucus than in joint session.

EVALUATE AND CHOOSE OPTIONS

When generating options, the assumption is that at some point the options will be evaluated jointly by the parties. Methods that help accomplish this include the following:

- *List of strengths and weaknesses.* For each option being considered, create a list of strengths and weaknesses (or advantages and disadvantages). The mediator turns to the list of options:

> We've got quite a number of possibilities listed here. Let's begin looking at them one at a time, starting with the first idea. What do you see as the strengths and the weaknesses of the suggestion that the state legislature should fund low-income housing in the area?

This process continues for each idea on the list. One way to record responses is to create a chart with a line down the middle. One side is for the strengths or advantages of an option, the other is for the weaknesses or disadvantages. Another method is to leave some space between each option when you are in the generating step so it is easy to go back and write the advantages (+) and disadvantages (–) beneath each option.

- *Cost-benefit analysis.* This approach is similar to the list of strengths and weaknesses, but the emphasis is on costs and benefits.

- *Establishment of criteria.* Before evaluating the options, agree as a group on essential criteria for any solution—for example, "We agree that the ideal solution would (a) develop a broad base of support for the housing initiatives, (b) involve low-income families in the decision making, and (c) spread the funding responsibilities among several sources." These criteria are normally close to the parties' underlying interests, and when they are identified, the choice of solutions becomes much easier. This approach is particularly useful in complex conflicts.

- *Anticipated impact exercise.* For each option, describe how this choice would affect the people involved. This helps objectify emotional discussion about why a course of action is or is not acceptable.

PROBLEM SOLVING AS A TRANSFORMATIVE PROCESS

This chapter has described activities to help parties find practical solutions to their problems. Where, then, does the possibility of lasting change in relationships or capacity of the individuals come in? In fact, many elements of transformative practice are embedded in the activities described here. Listening empathetically to parties, assisting them in listing their key issues, drawing them out to reflect on their underlying interests and needs, inviting them to propose solutions and evaluate them—all are activities that can *empower* the parties, which we identified in Chapter One as a central component in transformation. Engaging in these activities also offers participants constant opportunities for *recognition.* The mundane quality of these activities demonstrates the reality that transformation is a *process,* not an event. No magical techniques are capable of transforming the parties.

The whole process could quickly become nontransformative, however, if the mediators relax their commitment to transformation as their highest purpose. The greatest temptation usually comes from the mediators' inner needs for credit, success, or recognition. A mediator who gets anxious about not securing agreement, for example, will experience powerful urges to begin pushing the parties to accept one or another solution. The parties may even accept such an agreement and achieve "settlement." But if the agreement is based on mediator pressure and cajolery, and not on increased empowerment and recognition, transformation has not taken place. That may be better than no agreement at all. Or it may be worse, if the agreement falls apart in a few months because the parties felt no sense of ownership or if the settlement locks them into solutions with which they are uncomfortable.

The goal of transformation invites mediators to examine ourselves. Being aware of transformation in our own lives makes us more effective catalysts of transformation in others. Do we acknowledge our own gifts and abilities and use these to reach our full potential? Do we seek to empower those around us on a daily basis? To what extent do we recognize the intrinsic worth of other people? If we seek to be transformative, mediators must be prepared for a personal journey that reaches well beyond a set of techniques at the mediation table.

APPLICATION EXERCISES

1. In the following examples, the parties have made demands.
   - A group of students is demanding the resignation of the school principal.

- A company announces it intends to shut down one of its plants due to major financial losses over the past five years.

- In this same impending shutdown situation, the union calls for a boycott of all company products.

- In a conflict between two colleagues in a community organization, one person insists that her colleague, who has demonstrated poor management of funds in the past, be relieved of any duties in handling money.

Choose two or three examples that are of special interest to you, and answer the following questions:

- What might the interests or concerns underlying the demands be? In some situations, it might be more helpful to ask the question this way: What might be the problem (or the underlying interest) that the proposed solution (the demand) is intended to solve?

- In addition to the solution already proposed (that is, the demand), what other solutions could meet the underlying interests and needs of these parties?

2. Practice with a partner the art of interacting with someone who is taking a very demanding position in a conflict. Your task is to try to interact with this person in such a way that the focus of the discussion shifts from the person's demands or positions taken to the interests or needs underlying the demands.

In this exercise, take the role of a helpful facilitator or mediator who is trying to gain some insight into the perspective of a person in conflict. Your partner can choose an example from the situations in Application Exercise 1 or from personal experience. When you are finished, discuss the conversation. What strategies on your part were effective in helping someone in conflict move beyond initial demands to think about underlying interests and a variety of ways to meet them? Are there strategies you discovered that do *not* work?

CHAPTER 8

Additional Tools
for Problem Solving

ONE POSSIBLE SEQUENCE of activities for problem solving was introduced in Chapter Seven. This chapter suggests additional tools with a focus on defining problems and breaking impasse. The community peacebuilder's goal of transforming damaged relationships and unjust structures, not simply ending a specific conflict, makes additional tools particularly important. If mediators have a wide range of tools available to them, the chances are greater that they can find a strategy capable not only of resolving the issues at hand but also building a base for long-term transformation.

TOOLS FOR DEFINING PROBLEMS

As a general principle, it pays to define problems before trying to solve them. In Chapters Six and Seven, for example, mediators were encouraged to *formulate a list of the essential issues* that emerged in the Storytelling Stage before moving into the Problem-Solving Stage, where the parties begin discussing what to do about these issues. Mediators will be most effective if they know several methods for defining problems.

Joint Problem Analysis

This method is based on the assumption that the more clearly a problem is understood, the easier it is to solve. The goal is to help the parties jointly analyze the problems they face. The key to this method is that the mediators propose—and the parties agree—that during the discussion there will be no bargaining and no discussion of solutions. Rather, the focus will be on one or all of the following:

- How this situation affects us

- What matters most to us in resolving this problem

- Why this situation has been difficult for us
- Factors or criteria we will use in deciding whether solutions are acceptable
- Our fears or anxieties regarding this situation
- Our needs in this situation

Problem Definitions

Individuals write out definitions of the problem and hand them in. The facilitator reads these aloud, and discussion follows.

Separating Causes from Symptoms

The purpose of this method is to sort out which aspects of a problem are *causes,* and therefore merit serious attention, and which are *symptoms,* and therefore probably deserve less attention, as they are likely to disappear when causes are addressed. The procedure is as follows:

1. The mediator assists parties in jointly creating a list of problems or areas of concern.

2. With input from the parties, the mediator goes over the list and marks with a *C* all concerns deemed to be causes and with an *S* concerns deemed to be symptoms. Just because something is a symptom does not mean it should be ignored. Symptoms can cause a lot of damage! However, symptoms usually merit a onetime remedy, not long-term planning and change.

3. The parties help the mediator number the items on each list according to order of significance.

Phased Approach

In complex conflicts that require several meetings due to extreme polarization or numbers of people involved, it may be wise to agree to approach mediation in phases.

The first phase is *joint education* or information gathering. During this phase, the focus of discussion is on jointly educating each other about the facts of the situation and the perceptions of the parties involved. Mediators should point out that it is not necessary for the parties to agree on the facts of the situation. It is more important that all parties are fully informed about how the other parties view the situation, regardless of whether they agree with that view or not. This emphasis helps reduce the tendency to argue with other views. Joint education offers a way to ease into the issues; build relationships; identify structural economic, social, political, or administrative problems; and set the stage for later conversations.

The second phase is *problem definition.* During this phase the parties develop a list of "problem statements" that describe, nonjudgmentally and as specifically as possible, the problems that need to be addressed in order to resolve the conflict. Alternatively, the problem statements could describe the parties' *interests or needs* that have to be addressed to resolve the conflict.

The third phase is the *options generation* phase. Here the emphasis is on creating a list of options for resolving the previously identified problems.

The fourth phase is the *options evaluation* stage, during which the parties analyze each option according to strengths and weaknesses or costs and benefits.

The fifth phase is the *recommendations* phase, when the parties jointly choose the best solution to the situation and make recommendations about it.

The final stages are *implementation* and *evaluation.*

TOOLS FOR BREAKING IMPASSE

The school principal and the local chairperson of the teachers union had been arguing for an hour and a half. Both were entrenched in their positions. Thomas and his co-mediator, Miranda, were discouraged. Thomas thought to himself, "It looks like there's no way to avoid a teacher strike. Isn't there anything else we can try here before giving up?"

What would you do if you were in Thomas's shoes? Before reading on, stop for a minute and decide.

One important response Thomas can make to this difficult situation must take place in his own head. He will function more effectively, with greater confidence and calmness, if he recognizes that the mediators cannot make peace. Only the parties can. Of course, the mediators can assist in the discussion process, but in the end, it is the parties' conflict, and they are responsible for the outcome. The following tools help mediators move beyond an impasse and help the parties retain ownership of the outcome.

Avoid the Trap of Overresponsibility

Mediators who feel overly responsible for the outcome of a conflict function poorly in their role. If things go well, overresponsible mediators often seek personal credit for success, thereby arousing resentment in the parties and reducing their sense of empowerment. If things go poorly, overresponsible mediators often become frantic. Rather than being a quieting center that draws the parties beyond angry demands, these mediators feed tension and fear by bringing their own anxiety into the process. Desperate to avoid failure, they overreact to each difficult turn and begin pushing the parties to accept the mediators' suggestions for resolution. The parties usually resist this pressure, and before long the mediators find their energy consumed by arguments between themselves and the parties.

To the extent that mediators act in ways that suggest they feel *over-responsible* for resolving a conflict, the parties often react by becoming *under-responsible*. If the parties sense that the mediators feel responsible to come up with solutions and push hard for their acceptance, the parties tend to assume a passive or even negative stance. A situation quickly develops in which the mediators earnestly put forward solutions that the parties immediately reject, each party expecting that the mediators will pressure the other party into accepting a solution more favorable to its own position.

If the mediators recognize what is happening and know how to change their own behavior so that empowerment and responsibility pass back to the parties, the dynamics often change. Passing responsibility for resolution back to the parties usually involves adopting a relaxed attitude toward whether or not the parties can ultimately agree. Mediators focus their energy on drawing out the parties about their interests and needs, their options for responding to the situation, and the implications of those options.

In its strongest form, shifting responsibility can be expressed in a friendly query about ending mediation:

> It appears that neither side is prepared to take any steps toward the other to resolve things, and I'm not sure I can do anything further in this situation. Therefore, I want to hear from you about what to do. Do you want to continue this discussion, or is it time for me to withdraw and allow you to deal with the situation as you see fit?

The usual response is a panicky "Please don't go!" Thereafter, the parties often begin taking a more reasonable stand. By refusing to become over-responsible for the lives and problems of others, mediators can often increase the likelihood that others will take responsibility for their own problems.[1] If the parties do not object to the possibility of the mediator's withdrawing, this is a sign that indeed there may be little further that the mediator can do, and it is time to end mediation efforts.

Trust the Process and Focus on Understanding

Rather than feeling personally responsible for providing solutions, experience teaches many mediators to trust the mediation process to bring solutions. They know that any process will have moments of difficulty; they also know that the only way to get to the ups is by going through the downs. If they can just keep the right kind of process going, solutions will usually emerge.

What, then, is the "right" kind of process? It is a process in which the parties feel confident that the mediators understand their needs and interests and grow increasingly confident about this as the mediation unfolds.

Doesn't each side need to feel that the *other* side understands it as well? Ideally, yes, but the mediator's demonstration of understanding the parties *in the presence of both sides* leads them to understand each other better. If mediators believe this, their task is easier than it seems. Rather than seeking to persuade or pressure parties or to "solve their problem," it is often more effective simply to seek to understand them thoroughly.

Part of the challenge for mediators is to ask questions that empower the parties to think through their own situation and to recognize the situation of others. Here are some questions that may assist in reaching these goals:

- What is most important to you in this situation?

- What are your greatest hopes and your worst fears in this situation?

- Help us understand as clearly as possible your fears (resentments, frustrations) about this discussion.

- What cultural issues or traditions are important to recognize in this situation?

- As a party to this conflict, what do you see as your options at this point? How do you feel about these options?

- Are there particular points, concerns, or feelings that you especially want the other parties to understand?

- Help us understand as clearly as possible where you agree or disagree with the other party.

- What would you see as the ideal solution here?

- Are you aware of how others elsewhere have resolved a situation like this?

- Even if we cannot agree on everything, are there particular points that you think we might be able to resolve?

- How would you like to proceed if we are unable to come to agreement today? What do you see as the benefits and the costs associated with that path?

- What do you think are the major concerns or goals of the other side?

- Are there points being raised by the other side that you recognize as legitimate?

- What hopes or fears have you heard coming through from the other party in this discussion?

Draw the Parties into Joint Information Gathering

This strategy is often used in group facilitation. Gathering information gives a new focus, changes the dynamics, offers the parties something immediate and practical about which to cooperate, and sometimes uncovers new grounds for resolution. The parties might together make a trip to the site of a disputed property or hear from a respected person with expertise related to the conflict. They might form joint subgroups—for example, one to gather information regarding relevant legal issues and another to examine financial issues. If the matter is a community conflict involving many people, they might agree to go together to hear the perceptions of others involved.

Switch from Problem-Oriented Tasks to People-Oriented Tasks

Mediation involves not only problem-solving skills for negotiating difficult issues but also relationship-building skills for working with people who are hurt, angry, and suspicious. Success requires a good sense of when to switch from one set of tasks to the other. When things get difficult, it may be time to make such a switch. For example, if the parties are stuck on how to resolve an issue, it might be useful to point out common ground and areas of agreement or to give each side an opportunity to express feelings and experience the empowerment that comes from being listened to by an attentive listener.

Suggest a New or Different Procedure

Sometimes it helps to set aside the problematic issues and try to reach agreement on the next steps in the discussion process. For example, two colleagues in a community organization could not agree on sharing secretarial services. The mediator suggested that they set this issue aside for a week. During this time, each person should make a list of activities and times secretarial assistance was needed. The parties agreed and found a week later that with the additional information in front of them, they could negotiate a plan to coordinate secretarial services.

Use Caucus

A caucus is a private meeting between the mediator and only one party. To keep things balanced, mediators usually caucus with both parties, first with one and then with the other. The caucus provides a welcome "security blanket" for mediators. Dealing with one party is much simpler than dealing with both parties at the same time. When things get too tense or difficult, a caucus is one way to maintain control.

Some mediators do most of their work in caucus, conducting round after round of "shuttle diplomacy" between the parties. A common practice in labor-management mediation, for example, is to book three rooms for mediation in separate parts of a hotel, one for each party plus one for the mediators. The mediators begin their work by calling both parties into the mediators' room and announcing the beginning of negotiations. They then dismiss the parties to their rooms and begin a lengthy period of shuttle diplomacy, calling the parties into the mediation room one at a time. After a period of hours or days, if the mediation has been successful, the mediators call the parties back into joint session, announce the agreements that have been worked out, and conduct a signing ceremony.

However, caucuses should be used sparingly. People who have experienced this form of mediation as one of the parties commonly express suspicion of the caucus method. "I never trust what the mediator is doing with those other guys behind closed doors," says a veteran unionist about caucus. Since empowerment of others to solve their own conflicts is an important goal of conflict transformation, peacebuilders should work in ways that increase the capacity of parties to deal with problems themselves in the future. Caucus often has the opposite effect. The parties have little contact with each other and wait to be called by the mediators, who engage in the hard work of finding solutions. This leaves little room for the parties to build trust or develop new skills and patterns for resolving future conflicts.

Despite its shortcomings, caucus is a powerful tool that is sometimes essential in maintaining control and making breakthroughs in times of impasse. Mediators should know how to use it effectively at those moments. Here are examples of how mediators might accomplish particular tasks in caucus:

• *To set up a caucus:* "We'd like to take a break now and meet separately with each of you. We call this 'caucus.' It's a time to talk privately about how you feel things are going and to see if we can come up with new ideas for resolving things. Whatever we discuss in this caucus is confidential, and we won't share it with anyone else unless you give us permission to do so. Party A, perhaps we'll begin with you." Establishing confidentiality as the basis of caucus discussion often makes the parties more willing to enter sensitive discussion with the mediators.

- *To open discussion with one party during the caucus:* After Party B leaves the room, mediators might begin the caucus by saying, "Well, Party A, how do you feel about how things are going?" This gives members of Party A an opportunity to say whatever is on their mind or to discuss their feelings about what has happened so far in the mediation.

- *To discuss an issue that has caused special problems:* "Tell us more about your concerns regarding issue X. What is most important to you here?" This approach communicates concern for the party and gives the party a chance to talk about underlying interests.

- *To empower a party to think through options:* "What do you see as your options (or alternatives) in this situation?" "What do you see as the advantages and disadvantages of each of those choices?"

- *To seek fresh ideas for resolving an issue:* "Do you have any ideas that we haven't yet discussed for dealing with issue X? What do you think will happen if we don't get this issue resolved today? How do you feel about that? Is there any other way we can solve this?" The mediators try to get the party to come up with additional ideas rather than "selling" their own ideas.

- *To encourage each side to recognize the legitimate needs and interests of the other side:* "Are there needs or concerns raised by the other side that you see as valid or legitimate? To what extent are you prepared to cooperate in meeting those?"

- *To explore a particular solution with one party:* If mediators are unsuccessful in drawing positive suggestions for resolution from the parties, they may need to put forward some ideas. This should be done with "a light touch" to avoid a situation where the solution appears to be the mediators' rather than the parties' freely chosen response. "What if . . . ?" "Have you ever considered . . . ?" "In some situations, people have used the following as a solution. Do you think something like this would work here?"

- *To explore with one party a possible solution that the other party has proposed or already agreed to in caucus:* Usually it is wise to test out the acceptability of this solution with the other party without revealing that the first party has agreed to it. For example, "Supposing that we could get the first party to make a commitment to solution X, what kind of a response might you be willing to make?" The mediator knows, of course, that the first party is favorable to solution X but does not reveal this until permission has been granted from the first party.

- *To bring the parties into joint face-to-face discussion of things already discussed and agreed to in caucus:* Bringing the parties back into joint session, the mediator says, "Well, both of you have indicated some flexibility regarding issue X, and I'd like to have some joint discussion on this now. Party A, you have indicated flexibility regarding . . . , and Party B, you have suggested . . . I'd like to give each of you a chance to respond to this." Note that the mediator does not have either party "announce" to the other party that it is prepared to do Y if the other party is prepared to do Z. This is risky, as it may suggest that one side is trying to dictate the terms of an agreement to the other. If one side unilaterally wishes to announce an offer or a concession, that is fine. But if the proposal is a package deal requiring concessions from both sides, it is better for the mediator to summarize the proposal, say that both sides have indicated some interest in it during caucus, and then invite response from each side.

APPLICATION EXERCISES

After studying this chapter, consider the following questions.

1. Which approaches did you find the most helpful? Why?

2. Which ones were you most uncertain about?

3. What additional approaches to problem solving do you find effective?

4. What approaches to solving problems are valued by your tradition or culture?

5. How do your traditional approaches differ from those suggested in this chapter?

CHAPTER 9

The Agreement Stage: Seeking Sustainability

THE MEDIATION SESSION begins on a difficult note, and for the first hour, the mediators struggle to maintain control. Then a breakthrough takes place. It occurs on a minor issue, but the atmosphere changes, and by the end of the third hour, even the major issues have been resolved. The parties are relaxed, and before long it will be time to conclude the mediation session.

These mediators are entering a critical phase in the mediation process. The discussion has been successful, and strong temptations exist to relax a few minutes too soon. "Caution! Proceed with care!" is a warning signal that ought to be flashing in the mediators' minds at the point that success seems to be at hand.

Relaxing too soon can be costly. A common cause of failure in mediation is that mediators and parties neglect to work out the details and procedures for implementation of agreements. The result: days or weeks after an apparently successful settlement, renewed conflict may break out over the meaning of the original agreement. Sometimes this conflict can be resolved with another round of mediation, but often the agreement breaks down entirely, with the parties blaming each other for failing to keep promises. Peace may now be harder to achieve than ever; the parties will say they tried talking, and it does not work due to the craftiness of their opponents. By staying on guard to the very end of the session, mediators can greatly reduce the chances of such a scenario. By helping develop a clear, fair, and mutually beneficial agreement acceptable to all parties, mediators can lay the groundwork for transformed relationships.

TIPS FOR WRITING THE AGREEMENT

Be Clear, Specific, and Balanced

It is wise to avoid ambiguous words (for example, *promptly, soon, reasonable, cooperative, neighborly, frequent, quiet*) that may mean different things to different people. Use specific words and dates that leave as little room for misunderstanding as possible. Also make sure that both parties have assumed some responsibility for addressing the problems. Here is an example of a clearly worded agreement:

> *Mrs. Wrangle and the McBickers agree to build a six-foot-high board fence along the property line between their houses. Mrs. Wrangle agrees to pay the first $150 for building materials, and any additional costs will be split between the two families. The McBickers agree to construct the fence. Mrs. Wrangle will purchase the lumber for the fence no later than May 8, and the McBickers will finish the fence by May 30. Both parties agree to have their own side of the fence painted by June 30.*

There may be exceptions to these guidelines, of course. Sometimes mediators intentionally "paper over" differences with vague words in order to achieve agreement. However, this is justifiable only when there is reason to believe that the differences hidden in vague words can be dealt with more readily in the future than at the present moment.

Be Realistic

Mediators should be alert to promises that cannot be kept. For example, in one negotiation, the chairperson of a community organization was discussing an end to a rent strike and promised that all rent in arrears would be repaid within one month. The mediator knew, however, that many people who lived in the apartment building had no savings from which to make the substantial payments required. He raised this concern with both parties, inquiring whether they felt confident that the promise was realistic. After discussion, both sides agreed that the community group was not in a position to guarantee payment on behalf of people who were not present. Instead, the chairperson agreed to make a public call in the following week for an end to the strike and to cooperate with the building's owner in recovering unpaid rent.

If mediators have questions about the ability of parties to live up to the commitments they are making, they can raise their concern without insult by asking the parties to discuss how the agreement will work and whether they can think of anything that might cause problems with the agreements they are making. Alternatively, mediators can meet separately in caucus with the parties and raise concerns privately.

Be Proactive

Even the most carefully worked out agreements encounter problems in implementation. If the parties agree on a procedure to handle such difficulties, it is easier to prevent a total breakdown later. Even if mediators have no reason to question the sincerity of an agreement, it is wise to ask the parties how they would like to deal with problems that may arise in future. This is usually an easy matter to handle at this stage of the discussion, and whatever procedures are worked out can be included in the agreement itself.

Procedures to deal with problems that may arise in implementation of agreements could include any of the following:

- The parties agree that if difficulties arise, they will contact each other directly or through designated representatives.

- The parties agree to a date now for a meeting in the near future to review how things are going and to address any problems that have arisen.

- The parties agree to form a joint committee to oversee the implementation of the agreement and address problems as they arise.

- The parties agree that in the event of problems, they will immediately contact the mediator and schedule another mediation session.

- The parties agree that they will submit to an arbitrator or panel of arbitrators any conflicts that arise later and cannot be resolved through mediation.

Be Fair and Equitable

If the goal is conflict transformation, the parties need to feel good about the decisions made. If the mediators believe one party is being taken advantage of, they may be doing a favor for both by asking how that party feels about the agreement. In some circumstances, it may be wise to suggest that parties consult lawyers, accountants, or other specialists before finalizing agreements. Parties may meet separately with their own consultants or jointly with the same one. An unfair agreement seldom leads to sustainable peace.

Build Up the Relationship Between the Parties

Agreements can include steps to restore or strengthen relationships. Indeed, the mutual understanding developed in mediation and the confidence parties gain in their ability to handle future conflicts may be as significant as the actual resolution of a specific conflict. Mediators can foster ongoing transformation between the parties by inviting them to consider options for continuing to work on their relationship. For example, a mediation agreement between neighbors quarreling over dogs and children might include an invitation to dinner by one party to the other and an invitation for the children to come for ice cream and get acquainted with the dogs.

PRESENTING THE AGREEMENT

After working out the specifics of an agreement with the parties, mediators should summarize and review the proposed agreement with the parties and ask for their response. Does it accurately reflect the discussion that has taken place? Does it cover all essential issues? Do they pledge to live up to it?

Unless there is good reason to do so, leave no room for conflicting interpretations of what was agreed to in mediation. Often this calls for drafting a written agreement signed by both parties. Areas lacking clarity often become apparent only as one begins writing out the agreement on paper. A written agreement is more likely to be remembered by the parties and in many circumstances adds legal standing as well.

Sometimes it is desirable to prepare a nicely typed agreement for formal signing later. In this case, many mediators develop a handwritten draft at the mediation table and get the parties to initial it before ending the session. This draft can then be retyped and a formal signing ceremony scheduled for another time. Written agreements should be drafted in clear, straightforward language that is easily understood by the parties who will sign it. If you decide not to use a written agreement, take special care to summarize the agreement orally for both parties. Ask each party to respond by making a statement of commitment to the other party in response to your summary of the agreement.

WHEN NOT TO FINALIZE AGREEMENTS

Sometimes someone in mediation gets carried away with the success of talks and tries to move too quickly toward a resolution. This is especially a concern when an agreement will have an impact on people who are not present. For example, in a community dispute between a property owner and renters, it could be disastrous if the spokesperson or negotiator for the renters makes a final agreement without consulting the renters. They may resent being bound to an agreement in which they had no say. If they feel the negotiator has given away too much, the renters may view him as a traitor and disregard promises he has made. In the end, the situation could be more confused and conflicted than ever.

Nothing is worse for the prospects of peaceful resolution of a conflict than a breakdown in trust between negotiators and their respective constituencies. Unfortunately, negotiators often neglect their responsibility to maintain the trust of their constituents through frequent consultations. Mediators should be vigilant throughout the mediation process to protect and strengthen this trust.

Thus sometimes it is important not to finalize an agreement too early. Mediators should be cautious whenever people not at the table are significantly affected by a conflict or resolution. Sometimes it is wise to ask the parties, "How will your friends or constituents respond to the proposals we seem to be agreeing on today?" "Would it be wise for you to consult with them before formalizing our agreement?" "Is there any need to bring others into this discussion before we announce the progress we have made?" It can be difficult and frustrating to deal with the complications that sometimes emerge in such a consultation process. But these frustrations are small compared with the difficulty of repairing the damage when negotiators lose the trust of those they represent.

PROVIDING OPPORTUNITY FOR RECONCILIATION

Frequently, mediation helps disputing parties work out a practical solution to a problem without directly addressing the relationship between the people involved. Mediators should be alert for chances to invite the parties to take steps that will directly continue the reconciliation process. In some situations, these steps may be included in the agreement, as in the dispute between neighbors about dogs and children. In others, particularly where the atmosphere has turned strongly positive, mediators might invite the parties to speak to each other about the past.

In a conflict between co-workers, Barney, the mediator, realized that there had been a lot of resentment on both sides in the past and that both Lindy and Sam seemed to be feeling good about the discussion. He decided to take the discussion one step further. After the agreement had been signed, he said, "Lindy and Sam, one more thing before we end. This conflict has caused problems for both of you, and it sounds as though there have been quite a few angry words exchanged. If either of you wishes to say anything that might help put that behind you, I'd like to give you opportunity to do so now."

There was silence for a moment. Then Sam said, "Well, Lindy, I think we've made a lot of progress here—more than I expected. I admit that I was pretty angry with you these past few months, and I probably did and said some things that I shouldn't have. But I want you to know that so far as I'm concerned, that's behind us, and that I'd like to work cooperatively from here on."

Lindy listened thoughtfully and responded, "Sam, you did say some hurtful things. I said some pretty nasty things too. I'm ready to move on and make things better in the future." The two shook hands.

Barney concluded by saying, "You've both worked hard to resolve things, and you deserve a lot of credit for the agreement you've worked out. I will bring a copy to each of you this afternoon. If you have any further problems, you know where to reach me."

In bitter, long-standing conflicts, genuine reconciliation is usually a complex process. The following chapter suggests additional approaches to help participants let go of the past.

APPLICATION EXERCISE

Look in the media for news of negotiated settlements that failed, or recall personal experiences with agreements that came undone. What appear to be the causes of the failure or breakdown of the agreements? Consider such factors as fairness, clarity, attention to relationship building, and whether any mechanisms existed to deal with problems in implementation.

CHAPTER 10

Moving Toward Reconciliation: Letting Go of the Past

A MAJOR PROBLEM in almost every situation of conflict is the past. Lies have been told, damage has been done, pain has been inflicted, resentments have been aroused, and injustices have been perpetrated. How can peacemakers contribute to the necessary task of letting go of this history?

In 1991 I had the opportunity to attend the first multiracial gathering of religious leaders ever held in South Africa. The group of two hundred fell into a deep hush as a well-known white professor of theology ended his speech on the first day with an apology: "I wish to ask forgiveness for my role in the creation of apartheid, a system which I now believe to be sinful." Wiping his eyes, the professor sat down.

Appearing as surprised as the audience, the bishop who was presiding over the meeting made moves to close the session and proceed with tea, as scheduled. But just as people were beginning to rise to their feet, a short man in a cleric's collar hastened across the front of the room to the microphone. It was Archbishop Desmond Tutu. "We have been asked for forgiveness," he said. "Our Lord taught us to forgive. And I say to you, my brother, I forgive you." With these words, the meeting ended.

Twenty minutes later, I found myself walking with other delegates to the location that had been assigned for small group discussion of the morning's events. I sat down full of eagerness, feeling that a major watershed had just been passed and hopeful that further steps toward restoration between South Africa's diverse people might follow here.

"Wasn't that terrible!" said a mixed-race woman as we sat down. "I knew this was going to happen," agreed a black pastor sitting next to me. Stunned, I listened in silence as the members of my group, most of them victims of apartheid, criticized a confession that I had thought to be a constructive step forward.

As I listened, I learned much about the complex nature of the task of reconciliation from bitter conflict. My colleagues in the group viewed the confession as a bid for cheap grace. "They've taken everything from us," one member said. "Now they think that all they need to do is say they're sorry, and we'll say 'you're forgiven' and then they can go back to their comfortable lives released of all further moral obligations." Another added, "I don't want nice apologies so that white people can feel good. What I want is for whites to join us in the struggle to dismantle apartheid and create justice."

The skepticism expressed by people of color highlights an important reality for any discussion about healing from the wounds of the past. Reconciliation is often a long journey of transformation, not a single event. It is not just a matter of saying nice words and having pleasant feelings. Reconciliation requires facing the damage and hurt of the past, hearing the anger and resentment of those who are injured, and helping undo, wherever possible, the damage that has been done. Some of the steps in the journey of reconciliation are scary and painful and appear to take us backward. But often there is no way to continue with the journey unless we are prepared to take these steps, believing that they will ultimately lead to a good outcome.

TELL AND RETELL

One of the most important moments in the journey of reconciliation is when people are able to express anger, hurt, and resentment. If people are blocked from expressing these emotions, they may "freeze" in the healing process and find it difficult to move on. At the other extreme, however, uncontrolled expressions of anger may lead to a breakdown of the mediation process.

Often it is effective to maintain a positive attitude toward emotions as they surface in parties to conflict, acknowledging them without judgment and looking for ways to enable further expression of them in "safe" ways.

"In order to heal, a wound must first be cleansed." These words by a member of South Africa's Truth and Reconciliation Commission express a powerful truth about healing. For many people, the most important step toward healing is telling the story of hurt to an attentive listener. Despite what many people believe, telling stories of hurt does not reinflict injury. On the contrary, it is the story never told that holds people in secret bondage to old and festering wounds. By telling stories, people reassert ownership over their lives. Giving an angry or traumatized person the opportunity to tell the whole story about his or her trauma is a major contribution to that person's healing. However, storytelling is healing only if it is accompanied by careful, nonjudgmental listening. Peacebuilders need to cultivate the ability to listen with great attentiveness, setting aside judgment, as a fundamental skill in contributing to healing.

Each retelling provides the injured person with an opportunity to move another step forward in the journey of healing, away from the pain of the past to the possibility of renewed life and dignity in the present. Putting the pain into words helps affirm that the moment of injury is past. Although the results of the injury still linger, life continues in new ways, with other people, in the present.

Stories of deep trauma often need to be told many times in order to achieve healing. In normal daily life, someone who has been in a car accident, for example, will recount the experience repeatedly to sympathetic family and friends in response to queries about a bandaged arm. Such retelling serves an important emotional purpose in gaining release from the trauma of the experience. In some circumstances, mediators must be prepared to spend time in separate sessions with hurt and angry people to hear them out or to assist in finding someone who can serve in this listening role. To be a healing listener demands much from the listener, not only skill but also a sense of hope and a commitment to a potentially lengthy process. Remember that the goal of retelling is not to help people "forget the hurt" but to free them from its control.

ADDITIONAL STEPS

Peacebuilders can ask two simple questions that sometimes bring constructive responses from people who are stuck in old hurt: "What, specifically, do you need to do that would enable you to move on from the past? What could others do?" Responding to these questions shifts people out of the passive, blaming "victim" role, a role that makes them permanently dependent at an emotional level on the people they resent the most. By describing what steps for healing they could undertake and stating what they need from others, people move toward empowerment and mastery over their own lives.

Rituals can also be a powerful resource in assisting people to move through healing processes. Ritual provides a pathway through which people can channel negative emotions safely and open themselves up to new possibilities. Traditional societies were steeped in ritual, but under the influences of modernization, many of these rituals are falling into disuse. Peacemakers do well to explore the literature, dance, drama, song, poetry, liturgies, folk sayings, and ceremonies of cleansing and healing that lie within the cultural traditions of people in conflict. The wisdom and ways of the elders offer important resources for healing the wounds of their children and grandchildren.

APPLICATION EXERCISE

The opening paragraphs of this chapter describe reconciliation as a journey of transformation. It is useful to identify the steps on that journey and discuss them with other people. With one or two trusted dialogue partners, reflect on a personal experience of being hurt or angry with others. What is the sequence of stages you went through in order to move beyond alienation? What did you need from others (family, friends, colleagues) in order to assist in moving through each phase?

There should be no pressure to share more deeply than the speaker feels comfortable with. Each person needs to take responsibility to listen carefully and without judgment and resist the urge to give advice while others are describing their experiences.

After each person has had a chance to share, use these experiences to develop some guidelines about how (or how not) to interact constructively with someone who is angry or hurt.

Section Three

Communication Skills and Tools

CHAPTER 11

Listening Skills

ONE OF THE DEEPEST human needs is to feel understood and accepted by others. In their hearts, most people believe, "I may not be perfect, but I'm doing the best I can in a difficult situation." They long for others to recognize and respect how sincere they are in their attempts to do well against the complexities of life.

In conflict, people often use this deep need in others as a weapon. "You are not only mistaken, you are malicious, you are intentionally wronging me" is the message people who are angry often communicate to others. The messages of rejection may not always be sent in words. They are sent with equal clarity through tone of voice, gestures, and actions.

Anyone who has ever been falsely accused knows how painful and threatening the denial of understanding is and how strongly most of us react to this universal weapon. We react strongly because our very existence as social creatures depends on being understood and accepted by others. Our power to live and act and find meaning depends on being understood by others. When even a small number of people deny us understanding and acceptance, we may feel that life at the deepest level is under attack.

When people feel they are not understood, they often respond with extreme measures, including emotional withdrawal, verbal aggression, even physical violence. Even when their response is not extreme, people who feel they are not being understood function less effectively, and their flexibility, creativity, and general problem-solving abilities are diminished.

In contrast, offering understanding to another person is a potent form of empowerment. Understanding offers life, for it affirms its recipient's place in the human community. One need not agree with others to empower them.

Acceptance can be made clear through eyes, body posture, and tone of voice that say, "I accept you as a credible person; I want to see the world as you see it." "I want to understand you and your interests and needs." From the moment they feel another person truly seeks to *understand*, people often begin dealing with problems and relationships more constructively.

Demonstrating understanding for others is an essential skill for the mediator in improving the quality of the parties' behavior during mediation. More than this, it is also a major step toward building a base of power as a mediator. Mediators do not need power *over* the parties or an ability to coerce them. They need to establish power *with* the parties in the form of cooperation in creating safe space and establishing constructive patterns of communication. The mediator's initial goal is for the parties to know they are understood *by the mediator.* Trying to get the parties to understand each other comes later.

Listening is the primary means through which human beings communicate understanding. Thus good listening skills are critical for mediators. They serve a particularly prominent role in the Storytelling Stage, but progress depends on the parties' feeling understood and accepted throughout the mediation process. Good listening serves many positive purposes:

- It meets the universal need to be understood and recognized by others.

- It creates a supportive environment that helps the parties relax and focus on issues.

- It builds rapport and trust between the mediators and the parties.

- It provides an important example for the parties of how they need to interact if they are to resolve the conflict.

- It moves the focus of the conflict beyond apparent impasse to the deeper needs that motivate each party.

Mediators are only as effective as their listening skills. That is why good listening is at the top of the list of skills needed for mastery in learning mediation. Two forms of listening that are especially valuable for mediators are *paraphrasing* and *summarizing.*

PARAPHRASING

The following conversation takes place at a mediation session between two colleagues in a community organization.

John: She's impossible to work with in a group setting. She dominates conversations and gets very upset if she doesn't get her way. I just can't work with her anymore!

Mediator: So you're very frustrated with her response in group discussions, and at this point you've given up on working with her.

John: Look, I'm not saying I can't do anything with her. We can still do the community service work together, and I'm open to cooperating in the fundraising project. But I won't work on the Executive Committee with her. I just can't stand the constant battles.

Mediator: You're prepared to work with her in most areas, but it's on the Executive Committee where you've become really discouraged about working together.

John: Yes, I just don't think I can take it anymore.

Mediator: Um-hmm. Well, that gives us clarity about where you stand on this. Mary, let's hear from you. How do you see this?

Paraphrasing is a powerful and transformative skill in mediation for a number of reasons:

- It communicates understanding to each party.

- It moves the conversation to deeper levels (a good paraphrase often brings forth more reflective responses from others, as in the example).

- It slows down the conversation between the parties, serves as a buffer between their statements, and assists them in expressing their own views.

- It can be used to "launder" vicious or insulting statements to make them less inflammatory while retaining basic points that were made.

- By repeating the content of comments with less emotion, it makes it easier for opponents to hear and understand each other's statements.

Paraphrasing is probably the most important and fundamental skill in this entire manual. Learning how to paraphrase effectively needs practice. A good paraphrase should follow these guidelines:

1. Paraphrasing is repeating in your own words what you understand someone else to be saying. This means that you keep the focus of your paraphrase on the speaker and not on you, the listener. For example, you can say, "You feel that . . ."; "The way you see it is . . ."; "If I understand you correctly, you're saying that . . ." Do *not* say, "I know exactly how you feel. I've been in situations like that myself" or "You know, my sister had something like that happen to her a couple of weeks ago. She . . ."

2. A paraphrase is a summary and should always be shorter than the speaker's own statement.

3. A paraphrase mirrors the meaning of the speaker's words but does not merely parrot or repeat them. For example, a speaker might say, "I

resented it deeply when I found out they had gone behind my back to the director. Why didn't they just come and talk with me and give me a chance to sort things out with them?" An effective paraphrase would be: "You were quite hurt that they didn't come directly to you to resolve things." It would *not* be an effective paraphrase to say: "You resented it deeply when you found out that they went behind your back to the director. You wish they had come and talked with you and given you a chance to sort things out with them." That's repetition, not paraphrase.

4. A paraphrase contains no hint of judgment or evaluation but describes what was said in a thoughtful and supportive way. It may describe not only issues but feelings as well. For example: "You were very unhappy when he . . ."; "So when he walked out of the meeting, you thought he was trying to manipulate you"; "So your understanding is that . . ." It would be a mistake, however, to say, "That doesn't sound like a very constructive attitude to me" or "It sounds like you had good reasons for doing what you did."

5. Pay attention to the impact that paraphrasing has on people. Experience suggests that 10 to 15 percent of people seem to prefer *not* to be paraphrased. In some cultures, paraphrasing may be perceived as disrespectful. Observe the reactions of those you are paraphrasing, and adjust your use accordingly.

Learn to paraphrase in ways that fit naturally into the flow of ordinary conversations. Some people have been taught to paraphrase by using a "crutch phrase" each time they paraphrase. For example, they may begin each paraphrase with "What I hear you saying is . . ." This is annoying and obtrusive. Phrases like this can be effective when used appropriately, but with practice, you will find that you seldom need them. Skillfully done, paraphrasing should be so unobtrusive that others are not even aware that any special skills are being used. Their only awareness should be that the person paraphrasing is a good listener who is trying hard to understand.

SUMMARIZING

A summary is similar to a paraphrase but is longer. Mediators can use a summary to review the key points that have been made by one party in a statement, thus communicating the sense that they understand the entire situation being presented by that person. A mediator who is summarizing might say:

> We need to hear your neighbor's account, but before doing so, I'd like to make sure I understand you correctly. As you see it, this conflict began five years ago on the day you moved into the neighborhood, and your neighbor did things that you felt were discourteous. Things have become worse recently, as your neighbor's children have grown bigger. You feel that your dogs are quite safe with children as long as the children don't do anything to aggravate them, and you'd like your neighbor to talk with his children about what they've been doing to the dogs.

Summarizing can be used not only after one person has spoken but also to summarize the content of a discussion every few minutes as a way of keeping the discussion focused. For example, at one point in a discussion between police and community representatives about difficult relationships, a mediator made the following summary:

> It seems like a couple of concerns are being raised here regarding police and community relations. The community representatives are saying that they feel that police protection is completely inadequate and that the attitude of the police toward community members is not constructive. The police say that they have substantially increased the number of patrols in the community and are trying hard to improve their relationships, but they feel that they lack the support of community leadership needed to earn the trust of community members.

The mediator watched the faces of the disputing parties carefully as she spoke to make sure that people felt comfortable with her summary. Observing several slight nods of approval, she proceeded.

> It sounds as if one of the things that both sides agree on is a need for improved relationships between the police and the community. Perhaps we could talk about this for a few minutes and get some ideas from both groups about what could be done to address this problem. Does anyone have suggestions?

Note that the mediator here used summary to accomplish something mentioned in Chapter Eight, highlighting common concerns or common ground. She used the summary to focus the group's attention on a common concern, and she moved skillfully from her summary to invite the group to offer ideas for resolving the problem.

BODY LANGUAGE

Have you ever had the experience of meeting someone, having an apparently ordinary conversation, and then going away thinking, "I can't put my finger on it, but something doesn't feel right about that person!" Maybe it was a stranger whom you felt suspicious about. Maybe it was a friend who you sensed was upset about something. Without being able to name it as such, you may have been reading *body language*. Although your mind was focused on the words in your conversation, your eyes and ears picked up other signals: the posture of the speaker, the shifting of an arm or leg, a quick downward glance, an unexpected tone of voice, an expression in the face. Despite the ordinary words of the conversation, you had an almost intuitive feeling about the other person that spoke to you more loudly than the words you heard.

Some researchers say that as much as 80 percent of communication is body language. In other words, posture, gestures, facial expressions, eyes, and tone of voice have more impact on a conversation than the actual words used. Mediators can increase their effectiveness if they develop the discipline of constantly monitoring body language.

Every culture has its own body language. It is important for mediators to think carefully about how to use body language so that the message "I am eager to hear and understand you" comes through in ways that the parties can hear. For example, for a large man to communicate attention and respect to a man of equal physical stature might call for full posture and voice, whereas the same approach might seem intimidating to a smaller person. In many American and European cultures, it is important to maintain frequent or steady eye contact to communicate that you are listening. In many African and Asian cultures, by contrast, prolonged eye contact is considered too assertive or intimate, and keeping one's eyes averted is a sign of respect. By paying attention to their own body language, mediators can better communicate respect and sincere interest to the speaker as well as reduce their chances of unintentionally insulting others. By learning to observe and understand the body language of others, mediators can gather useful information about how parties are responding.

LISTENING AS TRANSFORMATION

A major component of destructive conflict is the inability of people to interact in ways that satisfy both their needs and the needs of others. These needs are often not obvious because the fight appears to be for money, power, property, or other material things. What is often at stake, however, is a deeper quest for self-development, empowerment, and recognition by others. The challenge of peacebuilding is to interact with people in conflict in ways that not only address the physical issues at stake but also understand and meet the inner needs that drive and motivate them.

Of the many skills mediators use, perhaps none is so transformative as good listening. Good listening offers deep recognition, for it acknowledges and honors the uniqueness of another human being. Consistently employed by mediators, it functions as a moral beacon to the parties, modeling a kind of interaction they can use with each other if they so choose. Good listening also empowers, for it invites and supports others to express themselves fully and deeply.

The skills of good listening can be learned and practiced. But from a transformative perspective, listening is about more than techniques for hearing the words of a speaker. It is about connecting to the deepest concerns and intrinsic worth of that person. Skills may point us in the right direction, but they can take us only so far. The connection must come from the heart. In practicing the skills of good listening, we give opportunities for transformation to others. We also receive the priceless gift that accompanies deep listening: the transformation of our own hearts that comes with any disciplined effort to truly hear another.

APPLICATION EXERCISES

1. Learning to paraphrase comfortably and naturally comes from practice. Begin to use this skill on a regular basis at home, at work, and on the phone.

2. You can increase your awareness of body language by talking with friends, family, and acquaintances.

   - Ask people what messages they get from your body language.

   - Ask people whether you use your body well to communicate that you are really listening.

   - Ask someone to mimic your body language, imitating as much of your arm, leg, eye, and facial movements as possible, and even your voice, if possible.

   - Ask people from other cultures whether they are aware of any ways in which body language in their culture is different from yours. How do they communicate respect in their culture?

3. Think of a time when you felt not only heard but uplifted by the way in which someone listened to you. What qualities in the listener made this experience transformative?

CHAPTER 12

Language in Mediation

PEOPLE WHO TURN to violence usually do so because they have been unable to solve their problems or achieve their goals through peaceful means, normally by talking with others. In any conflict, part of the challenge for mediators is to move the focus back to words as a more constructive place of engagement. This calls for special abilities to work effectively with the way people speak about their needs, about each other, and about their joint problems.

MOVING FROM GENERALITIES TO SPECIFICS

People in conflict tend to think and speak in broad terms or generalities. They often focus on only part of a situation and assume that this reflects the entire situation. For example, if Fred is abrupt with a woman on the street, she may generalize from this experience and conclude that rudeness is one of his normal character traits. She does not realize that he is upset and worried because his boss just fired him.

In conflict, people usually generalize from the worst behavior of others and from the best of their own behavior. A man who sees an opponent being unkind to others on three occasions in one month is likely to believe that this provides ample evidence that the other person is unkind in general. If in the same month he also observes his opponent being helpful to others on three occasions, he is likely to ignore these incidents or to doubt that his opponent was sincerely trying to be helpful.

When it comes to themselves, people generalize in the opposite direction. If we do three nice things in one month to others, we see this as proof that we are thoughtful and sincere, for it fits our view of ourselves. If confronted with examples of our own unkindness, we are likely to dismiss our actions as rare exceptions that were justified by the circumstances. When citizens of another country kill our civilians in war, we declare them ruthless aggressors. If citizens of our own country kill *their* civilians in war, we say that was the unfortunate consequence of our having to defend ourselves.

Whether the conflict is between persons or between nations, the same dynamic applies: most people generalize from their own best intentions and behavior and from the worst behavior of those whom they mistrust. The result is a gap in perceptions that leads parties in conflict to be self-righteous and indignant.

The words people use to talk about their conflicts reflect this tendency to generalize:

These people have no respect for the rights of others.

He's got a real attitude problem; he thinks he's better than we are.

She is completely unreliable; she's always late, and she never keeps her promises.

He's a racist.

Of course, there may be elements of truth in each of these statements, but it makes things worse to characterize others in such broad terms. Broad generalities often perpetuate the behaviors to which the speaker objects because their use escalates anger and resentment.

Discussion seldom leads to resolution of a conflict as long as the parties speak in generalities. Only when the parties begin talking in specific terms about why they are unhappy or about their vision for the future does it become possible to negotiate a settlement. Changing attitudes is a difficult task, and it is seldom possible to accomplish this quickly. However, even a small shift in the words people use is often enough to enable a resolution of key practical problems. This shift in turn opens the possibility of larger, long-term changes in attitude.

Mediators can lead the way in this by getting the parties to speak in terms that are more specific. Careful use of open questions and statements inviting more information is the primary skill needed to accomplish this. Consider these examples:

North: He always comes in late.

Mediator: Can you give me an example of when he comes in late? *or* What is he late for? *or* Tell me more about that.

• • •

South: He's got a real attitude problem; he thinks he's better than the rest of us.

Mediator: Tell me about a situation in which you felt this way. *or* Give us a specific example.

•   •   •

East: That whole bunch is an irresponsible lot.

Mediator: Who specifically do you have in mind? *or* In what ways are they irresponsible? *or* Tell us more about that. *or* Give us an example.

•   •   •

West: He's a racist.

Mediator: Explain what you mean by that. *or* Tell us what he does that you are unhappy with. *or* Give us an example of something that happened that brought you to this conclusion.

Many different responses can move a discussion to the level of specifics. The key is that mediators should be able to recognize generalities and respond in a way that invites the speaker to describe the specific experience behind it.

LAUNDERING LANGUAGE

Because hostile, critical language used by one person can arouse hostility in others, mediators often need to reduce tension by "laundering language." This selective form of paraphrasing restates strong feelings in less emotional terms.

North: *(in reference to South, across the table)* This guy is lying through his teeth! What he's saying is complete nonsense! He was the one who came to my house, woke me up, and started shouting at me like an idiot! I never came near his house!

Mediator: So you disagree strongly with his account. Your memory is that he came to your house and the argument took place there, not at his place.

The mediator acknowledged the essential point but chose less inflammatory words to paraphrase the speaker's content. In laundering language, the mediator must paraphrase the essential content of the speaker's words and not simply gloss over the difference. Otherwise the party will object and repeat the original attack.

HEARING HIDDEN OFFERS

Because parties usually view themselves as sincere and well intentioned, they toss offers of peace into a discussion with surprising frequency. However, they often do so in such a way that even mediators do not notice them or in ways that their opponents would be unable to accept. For example, neighbors North and South are in a mediation session about a fence damaged by North's car. North says to the mediator, "If he'd stop acting like such an idiot, I would have fixed his stupid fence a long time ago!" *What is the offer implied in this statement?*

Here's another example. The director of a community center is in a mediation session with the caretaker, whom he has threatened to fire for not doing proper maintenance on the building. The director says to the mediator, "Listen, I'm not trying to be hard-nosed about this. I know very well that one maintenance man can't do everything! But how can we ever work things out, if he's not man enough to come and let us know what he can and can't do?" *What is the offer implied in this statement?*

In each case, the speaker hints at an offer for peace, but the offer is delivered in a wrapping of insults. Unless the mediator is listening closely and is skillful in untangling the hint of peace from the insults, the other party will hear only the insult, and the offer will fall away ignored. Careful paraphrasing is the mediator's most useful tool here.

In response to Neighbor North, the mediator could say: "You've been unhappy with some of the things he has done. However, if I understand you correctly, you're saying you are willing to fix the fence if his behavior toward you improves."

In response to the director, the mediator could say: "So you recognize that there are limits to what you can expect one person to accomplish, and you want to be reasonable about that. What is especially important to you, however, is that you have a clear understanding with the caretaker about the jobs that he can and cannot handle."

These responses acknowledge the anger and frustration reflected in the insulting comments. After all, if the mediator ignored the negative feelings completely, the speaker would probably continue repeating them. But in the mediator's response, the negative feelings are paraphrased in such a way that the insulting elements are "laundered out" and the positive elements are highlighted. The conversation can now continue around the offer that the mediator has just rescued from the trash bin of insults.

APPLICATION EXERCISES

Moving from Generalities to Specifics

1. Write a question or response that a mediator who hears the following statements could make to move the speakers from generalities to specifics.

    a. "They're jealous, that's the problem."

    _____

    b. "This guy is totally irresponsible. He has no sense of discipline or accountability to others."

    _____

    c. "She's the most uncooperative employee I've ever had."

    _____

    d. "People around here are cold and unfriendly."

    _____

    e. "Everyone on the block has trouble with him."

    _____

Laundering Language

2. "Launder" the following statements made by one party to a conflict about the other party.

    a. "All these people care about is power and money. That's the only thing that motivates them! They don't care who gets hurt in the process! Our side is trying to build up this community and make an attractive environment so our families have a decent place to live. All these people want to do is destroy this place."

    _____

    _____

    _____

b. "They think they can push us around! They think they own this place! Well, I have been a man of reason up to now. But we've got rights, and we are going to defend ourselves! If they cause any more trouble, I'm going to call my people into action, and we'll show them quickly who is stronger!"

_____

_____

_____

c. "Look, this business about racism is a complete crock that the union is manufacturing to harass us. The guy is just plain lazy; he couldn't do a proper day's work if he tried. That's why I want him out of here!"

_____

_____

_____

Hearing Hidden Offers

3. You are mediating between two parties, and you hear the following hidden offers made by one of them. Each statement comes from a different conflict setting. How would you respond? Write your response on the line.

a. "Look, we're prepared to be reasonable in this if she is. But so far the only thing we've heard from her is a bunch of excuses and accusations! Until she shows a different attitude, I don't see much point in this discussion!"

_____

_____

_____

b. "We don't want war in this neighborhood! I came here today because I'd like to talk peace and I'd like to go home and tell my friends to cool things. But these people sitting across the table are warmongers! They do whatever they think they can get away with! If they want war, we'll give them war!"

_____

_____

_____

c. "I'm a decent person! If any of my neighbors thinks my music is too loud, they can come and tell me and I'll turn it down. But they had better do it in a civilized manner! This guy *(nodding at the party across the table)* has no idea what that means. Why should I cooperate with someone who comes and shouts at me like an idiot? If he does it again, I'll just turn my music up louder!"

_____

_____

_____

CHAPTER 13

Emotions in Conflict

HOW PEOPLE DEAL with their feelings varies greatly from one culture to another. In some cultures, it is normal and expected that people in conflict will express anger or sadness freely. In others, direct or open expression of such feelings is viewed as disgraceful or deeply insulting. Nevertheless, one statement applies universally to all cultures: strong feelings play a prominent role in conflicts. Knowing how to recognize the presence of strong feelings and how to respond constructively is a crucial part of mediating or facilitating a discussion between disputing parties.

THE IMPORTANCE OF SELF-AWARENESS

Even people within the same culture deal with feelings differently. A mediator who tolerates outbursts of anger may seem irresponsible to one person; a mediator who does not allow such outbursts may seem artificial and repressive to another. Thus mediators need to adapt to the dynamics of each situation.

Adaptability begins with self-awareness. Unless we have a clear awareness of our own natural preferences regarding how to deal with feelings, we will assume that everyone functions the same way we do, and we will rigidly insist on imposing our own preferences on others. You may find the questions in the exercise at the end of the chapter useful in expanding your awareness of your own preferences for dealing with feelings.

A RANGE OF MEDIATOR RESPONSES

Let us look at some skills and strategies for dealing with emotions in mediation. These approaches vary significantly. Some actively encourage the parties to express their emotions; others discourage and restrict the expression of emotions at the mediation table.

Accept and Acknowledge Emotions

Because people are deeply influenced by their own emotions, it is often better to deal openly with feelings during mediation. What is out in the open is usually easier to work with constructively than what is hidden. Talking about feelings to an accepting listener reduces the power of those feelings. Mediators can deal constructively with strong feelings by listening carefully to and accepting someone who is angry or hurt and by using paraphrasing to acknowledge the feelings that have been expressed.

Regardless of the culture, listening well to parties who are upset and paraphrasing their feelings is likely to reduce eruptions of feelings later. What varies greatly is the acceptability of expressing emotions in meetings or in the presence of an opposing party.

Set Ground Rules

If anger is escalating to a level that threatens to block communication, it may be wise to propose ground rules and ask both parties to agree to them before continuing. For example:

> It seems there is a lot of anger here that is getting in the way of talking things through. I'd like to propose a couple of guidelines for the rest of this session. One is that there be no further name-calling. Second, I'd like to ask that you address your comments to me and not to each other during the rest of this discussion, unless I specifically ask you to do otherwise. I'd like to gain a commitment from each of you about this proposal before we continue.

Create a Structure for Discussion

Create a structure in which people can express their feelings without getting into arguments. You can do this with techniques such as taking turns and coaching the parties to paraphrase.

Take Turns

The mediator invites the parties to take turns talking about an issue or about their feelings:

> Both of you have mentioned an incident that took place last year when you had a public argument. It's clear that you have strong feelings about this, and it might be good to talk about that incident a little further. What I'd like to ask is that we agree to do this in turns, so that each of you has a chance to express your feelings without being interrupted. Perhaps we could begin with you, Mr. East, and I will ask you to address your comments directly to me. Mr. West, I'd like to ask you just to listen quietly for a few minutes, and then it will be your turn to speak.

East then tells his side of things, and the mediator paraphrases. The same process is repeated with West.

Taking turns can be used throughout mediation to maintain control during discussion of any topic that arouses strong feelings. Asking that the parties speak to the mediator rather than directly to each other also reduces the possibility of provoking an angry exchange.

Coach Paraphrasing

In this approach, the mediator guides the parties in paraphrasing each other, an exercise that can be remarkably powerful in helping parties let go of their feelings and encounter each other as people:

> It seems that a lot of strong feelings are blocking further progress in this discussion. It may be necessary to try to address these feelings before we can go any further. I'd like to give each of you a chance to listen carefully to the other person for a time and to do it in a special way. We'll begin with you, Mr. West. I invite you to speak to Mr. East about the things that you have resented the most over the course of this conflict. Mr. East, it will be your job to listen in this first round, and not only to listen, but also to summarize in your own words every few sentences what you hear Mr. West saying to you. This may be difficult at first, and I'll give you some help until you get a feel for what we are doing. When we have finished with the first round, it will be Mr. East's turn to speak and Mr. West's turn to listen and summarize. Many people have found this a powerful exercise, but it is difficult, especially for the one who must listen and summarize. Before we begin, I'd like to hear if you're willing to try this.

If the parties agree to engage in this exercise, it is almost impossible for them to retain their old feelings. Note that this approach will not work unless the parties really want to get past their resentment. If they want to rant and rave for a while, the technique will fail miserably. It is not for routine mediation or unsteady mediators, so use it with care.

Caucus or End the Session

If emotions seem to be escalating to a danger point, the mediator may wish to propose a fifteen-minute caucus (separate meeting with each party) or break or suggest that the session end and be continued on another day. During this interval, it may be wise to spend some time with each party privately to give them a chance to vent or express their feelings.

Use Shuttle Diplomacy

Working *exclusively* in caucus provides the greatest level of control over anger. In this approach, the parties have no face-to-face contact. Rather, the mediator shuttles from one party to another, taking ideas back and forth. It is most commonly used where the parties are too angry to agree to a face-to-face meeting or where the mediator fears that it may be impossible to prevent a destructive confrontation if the parties do meet. In order to help the parties build a more positive relationship and empower them to address future disputes more effectively, the mediator should look for opportunities to bring the parties together again for further discussion as soon as possible.

SUMMARY

The emergence of strong emotions in mediation tests the mediator. Are feelings an enemy or a friend in the task of peacebuilding? They can be either. In the right setting, the expression of strong emotions can be a transformative step for parties in conflict. If mediators are themselves comfortable with the reality of strong emotions in others, they can think flexibly about the critical question of whether to work with emotions in joint session or in one-on-one settings.

APPLICATION EXERCISES

Discuss these questions with another person:

1. What do you do when you feel angry, sad, embarrassed, or afraid? Do you grow quiet and withdrawn, or do you become expressive and vocal?

2. How do you respond when others are emotional? Are you comfortable with the expression of strong emotions, or do you prefer that people keep their feelings to themselves?

3. What life experiences have influenced the way you respond to emotions?

4. What moral guidelines and spiritual or cultural resources have shaped your own attitudes and habits regarding strong feelings?

Section Four

*Building Peace
in Communities*

CHAPTER 14

Designing a Peacebuilding Process

LIFE WOULD BE EASIER if all conflicts could be dealt with by gathering a few individuals around a table to mediate differences. Unfortunately, things are not that simple. Many conflicts involve large numbers of people in groups and organizations. Frequently, unjust structures or abuse of power are primary causes of such conflicts. Dealing with these complicated realities requires skills of social analysis, advocacy and activism, group leadership, and group empowerment. These are complex skills that lie beyond the scope of this book.

Nevertheless, it is important for mediators to see the connection between the skills they employ at the mediation table and the needs of groups and communities for just and peaceful resolution of more complicated conflicts. This final chapter examines the connection between mediation skills and the struggle for healthy communities and proposes that a common set of values and skills underlie peacebuilding in settings of both individual and group conflicts. The concept of transformative "process design" offers a set of guiding principles that apply to both individual and group peacebuilding efforts.

MEDIATION SKILLS AND THE STRUGGLE FOR JUSTICE

"What do I need mediation skills for? I'm a community activist! My job is to stir people up, not calm them down!" commented a community worker in a workshop. But when he stopped to think about it, this gritty organizer recognized that one of the biggest challenges he faced was conflict among the people with whom he worked. In the past year, three staff members had left his organization as a result of personal tensions among colleagues, and mistrust continued among remaining staff. In the community he sought to organize, a long history of suspicion and competition among groups holding differing political leanings prevented people from working together to address problems of racism, unemployment, and housing that plagued the entire community. Religious and service organizations worked in isolation from each other, each suspicious of the others.

Tragically, one of the first consequences of injustice is division among its victims. Go to almost any "oppressed" community and you will find deep, disabling, and sometimes murderous divisions between people who have every reason to call themselves brothers and sisters in the struggle for justice. In many communities throughout the world, these internal divisions are as grave an obstacle to the efforts of oppressed people in redressing injustice as the repression imposed on them from the outside. Repressive governments skillfully exploit the divisions in vulnerable communities to weaken the forces working for change.

For many years, justice workers have recognized, practiced, and taught the skills of activism and nonviolent confrontation. These skills deserve a prominent place in the repertoire of peacebuilding practice, for they can activate communities to exercise abilities that lay sleeping. But applied alone, they cannot bring sustainable justice, for they fail to address the realities of internal diversity and polarization that arise as efforts at social change progress, and they do not build the relational ties often required between former opponents. Empowerment of communities requires more than just arousing and mobilizing people; it requires forging and maintaining coalitions and bonds of unity. Without these, communities are unable to grow and to reach their full potential, for their energies are constantly fragmented and diverted in internal strife. The most empowering leader is one who is skilled both in activism and in mediating differences and is gifted in making a graceful transition from one mode of operation to the other.

EXTENDING MEDIATION VALUES INTO GROUP CONFLICTS

This manual offers tools to assist individuals in conflict to grow amid their differences, to empower them to think and act with greater strength, and to increase their capacity to recognize the realities and needs of others. At one level, these may be understood as mere techniques to assist human interaction. But in fact they are more than this. They are based on and support deep values about the human community and decision making. If we state these values explicitly, we can more easily extend them to the more complex arena of group conflicts.

We noted in Chapter One that conflict transformation is grounded in awareness of the uniqueness and intrinsic worth of every human being. Believing that every person is distinctive and of ultimate value has implications for how we relate to people.

We relate to others in ways that consistently recognize and honor the dignity and potential of each person. Whether mediating between individuals or facilitating a community meeting, for example, we treat each person with respect and discourage put-downs, name calling, or insults.

We take seriously the challenge of supporting persons with whom we work to reach for their fullest potential as human beings, and we interact in groups in ways that encourage others to do the same. For example, we invite people to express themselves fully and clearly in storytelling; we take their needs, goals, and hopes seriously; we encourage them to consider the full range of options available to them; and we expect them to make decisions about their own lives rather than wait for others to solve their problems.

Transformative mediation is interested, then, in more than solutions to conflict; it seeks to create a particular kind of interaction among human beings. Transformative mediators bring an agenda to the table: to help create processes of interaction that empower participants and foster recognition of their intrinsic worth. We pursue this agenda not by "taking sides" but by facilitating processes of interaction that support empowerment and recognition and by actively avoiding or blocking those that hinder them.[1]

THE POWER OF PROCESS

Peacebuilding with groups extends the same agenda to more complicated settings. The implications of this are easier to see if we recognize that peacebuilding in group settings is primarily about *decision making.* Emotions and conflicting perceptions are part of the picture as well, of course. But conflict involving numbers of people is usually driven by the belief that decisions have been made or are going to be made about matters or resources of concern to all. Thus we can view peacebuilding in group settings as *establishing or supporting decision-making processes that assist empowerment and recognition to take place in conflicts involving numbers of people.*

Work in group settings requires a clear grasp of process design, that is, of how to go about group decision making in ways that support transformative values. Process design begins with the recognition that there is a difference between *process* and *outcome,* between *how* and *what.* In particular, process design recognizes that in group settings, people are usually more sensitive about *how* a decision is reached than they are about *what* the decision is.

Outcome is the what, *the decision reached, or the result achieved.*

Process is the how, *the way in which a decision is reached.*

Consider the principle at an everyday level. It is time for a coffee break at a meeting of professional colleagues. The chair suggests a thirty-minute break, calls out the names of three women, and asks them to go and set up the refreshments. These women are all from the same racial group, a minority in the community and the professional group. During the break, others from this ethnic group gather in a corner and angrily discuss the double problem of sexism and racism. After the break, they confront the chair and the entire group.

In another organization, it is also time for a coffee break. Here, too, the leader announces the names of three minority women chosen to serve refreshments. However, here the women laugh good-naturedly as they rise to undertake their duties. Why? Their names were chosen randomly by "pulling straws." The *outcome* was the same in both groups—reluctant individuals were chosen to prepare refreshments. In the second group, however, the outcome was accepted because the *process* was fair.

Why are people so sensitive to process? Why do they often care more about the way in which a decision is made than about the actual outcome of the decision? Intuitively, people sense that process makes profound statements about human worth, about "who counts." Most people can accept surprising amounts of disappointment and frustration about not winning the outcomes or decisions they seek—whether those outcomes are political, financial, organizational, or technical—so long as they feel that the process was fair and respectful. But those same people will often rise up in bitter, defiant outrage if they feel that the way in which decisions were reached was unfair or demeaning.

"They act as though we don't even exist!" muttered an outraged community leader after city officials announced plans to sell several acres of an abandoned educational institution to developers, without consulting local residents. This leader may not have thought enough about decision making to say that assessments of human worth are implicit in the way all decisions are made. However, like most people, he was exquisitely sensitive to *bad process* when it was used on him. He saw that more was at stake than a mere decision about land use; he saw that failure to consult with local citizens about a decision that would alter forever the character of their neighborhood represented a fundamental attack on residents' having a voice in their own future. Along with dozens of other outraged neighbors, he mounted a campaign that unseated an entire group of officials in the next election.

A great deal of group conflict is simply the consequence of bad process, for people commonly reject even the best ideas and proposals if they are created in processes they find objectionable. On a daily basis, thoughtful and well-intended leaders violate principles of good process design in faith communities, schools and universities, and governmental and public institutions and are baffled by the reactions of others around them. These leaders are focused on outcomes that are often laudable. As a result, however, they may be unaware of the damage inflicted on relationships by processes that imply that others do not deserve to be consulted or involved in decision making. Often they find it difficult to understand why process is so important or to recognize the difference between good and bad process.

Most people find it easier to identify bad process than good process. For many years, we have asked people in workshops to tell stories about times when they were on the receiving end of bad process: "Tell about a time when you were upset, not so much about a decision, but about the way in which a decision was made. Explain why you were upset." Stories pour forth in response to this invitation. As groups reflect on these bad experiences, principles for good decision-making processes emerge that carry important insights for responding transformatively to group conflicts.

PRINCIPLES OF GOOD PROCESS

1. *Good process begins by asking, "Who should be involved?" not "What are we going to do?"* Who is involved in decision making or negotiation? The answer communicates much about "who counts." Beginning with "What are we going to do?" overlooks the extremely sensitive "who" question and alienates people whose support is essential to long-term peace. A commitment to the transformative value of empowerment suggests that the first step in making decisions is to determine who will be affected so as to involve them appropriately. Questions to guide in this assessment include these:

- Who will view themselves as deeply affected by this negotiation, project, or decision? (*This group should be at the heart of the decision-making process.*)

- Who is in a position to block implementation if they are unhappy with decisions? (*These parties should always be consulted and often need to take an active part in the decision process.*)

- Whose advice or assistance will be valuable? (*This question calls for broad consultation.*)

- Whose approval will be required to enable this project to proceed?

- What are the interests, concerns, or motivations of each of the groups just identified?

2. *Good process is conducted under auspices acceptable to all.* Who is viewed as "sponsoring" or "running" the decision-making or negotiation process? Parties tend to link sponsorship with whoever announces an event or invites people to it, who pays for it, who facilitates, who appears to be positioned to get credit if the event is successful. When mistrust is high, it is imperative that sponsorship be perceived by all as impartial, for sponsorship is rightly understood to increase the power and influence of the sponsor.

If a community is complaining about police brutality, a forum for dialogue between police and community is unlikely to earn community trust if it is sponsored solely by the police. Good process design would call for such a forum to be sponsored by an independent organization or jointly by the police and a trusted community organization.

If a congregation is deeply divided over styles of worship, the Worship Committee that has been advocating one particular style of worship is unlikely to be viewed as an impartial sponsor of a dialogue process. By *role*, the Worship Committee might appear to be the obvious sponsor, but parties do not trust processes sponsored solely by someone they distrust. The Worship Committee should invite another body in the church to sponsor the process or perhaps ask for a special committee containing representatives of the major views to be appointed as sponsor.

3. *Good process involves essential parties or their representatives, not only in negotiation and decision making, but also in the design of the process itself.* It is important to consult with primary parties early in planning a decision-making or negotiation process while process plans are still tentative. All too often, a small group of well-intentioned people plans a discussion or decision-making process and then goes to the parties and tries to "sell" it to them, soliciting their participation. This approach makes it difficult to recover from even small mistakes in strategy planning and fails in the transformative goal of empowering the parties.

Suppose you are the leader of one of two major groups involved in a community dispute over what to do with the vacant lot next door. You have been organizing your supporters for many months and lobbying city officials. One Saturday, you receive a polite invitation announcing that your chief opponent is convening a meeting at his house next Wednesday to "bring together responsible citizens in order to make decisions critical to the future of our community."

Would you go? You are likely to be less than thrilled about the invitation, given the lack of consultation. You also sense that if the meeting succeeds in bringing together key people from the community and enabling good discussion, your opponent will gain considerable stature as a consequence. Even if his motives are sincere, your opponent is unlikely to gain your participation or trust.

Imagine a different scenario. A group of local businesspeople announce they are gathering a "neighborhood commission" to make recommendations on the matter to the city council. Along with fifteen other people, you are asked to come to the first meeting, which will be chaired by two local businesspeople. How will you respond now? You wonder who these businesspeople think they are to suddenly put themselves in the role of brokering community decision making on a matter you and others have worked on for years. You have no idea who half the other people on the commission are. You do know your opponent hangs out in business circles, and you suspect that the people convening this are his friends.

To earn trust and participation of primary parties, peacebuilders should consult with them early in the planning of peace efforts and make them feel that they have helped design the negotiation process. Peacebuilders should go to them and say, "We are wondering about creating a forum in which people can talk. Would you be interested? What should it look like? Who should be there? When and where should we meet? Who should convene it? Should it be on the record or off the record?" Don't build and then try to sell a process to the parties. *Create one with them* in tentative, low-key private discussion before announcements of plans to talk are made.

Whether the conflict is in a religious congregation or a political ward, if the parties indicate an openness to talks, one way to design the process is to create a "process committee." Composed of thoughtful people from all key parties, this group has the task of planning, announcing, and coordinating the process of negotiation or decision making.

4. *Good process is clear about the purpose and expectations of each step and provides good information about the process.* A common cause of conflict is confusion about pivotal events.

- *The director of an organization appoints a committee to study staff salary structures. The committee makes a number of recommendations, which the director chooses to ignore. Staff are further polarized now, for many believe the director acted in bad faith. He says he never promised to accept the findings of the committee; that he viewed it as purely advisory.*

- *A vote is held in a religious community. A number of people say that they didn't come to the meeting when the vote was held because they*

> *thought the session was merely to exchange views. They thought the vote would be held in a month during the annual business meeting. This group agitates for a new vote.*

- *A newly formed committee agrees to put a critical issue to "majority vote." Sixty percent vote yes and claim they clearly won. Others say the measure lost, insisting that 67 percent is required for a majority. Both sides accuse the other of trying to manipulate the rules.*

Much dissension can be avoided if clear understandings about each step in the decision-making process are worked out in advance. As much of the overall process as possible should be mapped out early in planning. Parties should share common information on the *purpose* of the process, *what* will happen *when* (a timeline is helpful here), *who* will make the final decision, and *what decision-rule* applies (51 percent majority, 67 percent majority, consensus, and so forth). These issues cannot usually all be decided at the beginning of the process, but they should be clarified as early as possible. They should be decided in close consultation with the persons most deeply involved in the process and communicated clearly to all. If a process committee is set up as suggested in point 3, the first task of such a committee could be to bring to others a written proposal that makes recommendations in each of these areas.

5. *Good process offers more than one kind of forum to consider options and express opinions.* The goal is to ensure that all persons can contribute in a forum in which they feel comfortable. In institutional settings, use a mix of large group discussion, small group discussion, polls or questionnaires, study circles, and personal interviews. In community or political settings, in addition to these approaches, use conferences, community forums, publications, and study materials.

6. *Good process maintains trust through regular interim reports to the people affected.* During the negotiation or discussion process, use open forums, surveys, nonbinding votes, and questionnaires, and make sure the whole group knows the results so the trend of the discussion is clear to all before the decision is final. If people are shocked at the outcome of a decision-making process, it is usually a sign that the designers failed to build adequate interim reporting mechanisms into the process. Disappointment is normal in decision making and need not be a cause for worry. Shocked surprise is a different matter, for it often brings charges of unfairness.

Interim reports should achieve three objectives:

- They should summarize ideas, opinions, and suggestions gathered so far in the process through interviews, meetings, and written forms.

Gathering such information about people's views without reporting it back often leads to charges of manipulation.

- They should communicate decisions made by subgroups.
- They should give people frequent opportunities to comment about how they feel about the process, whether it is fair, whether they understand the next steps, and so forth.

7. *Good process cannot happen without careful thought, consultation, and planning.* Haste is a major enemy of good process and usually leads to great waste of time and energy in the end.

CONCLUSION: A TRANSFORMATIVE PROCESS FOR COMMUNITY EMPOWERMENT

This chapter highlights the connections between basic mediation skills and the requirements of complex conflicts. We assume that readers interested in working in more complicated settings already have or will acquire skills in such areas as assessment, group facilitation, structured dialogue, consensus-building, group dynamics, and organizational planning and development. These skills will enable peacebuilders to extend the values and skills found in mediation into a more challenging arena.

From a transformation perspective, the basic components for dealing with individual and group conflicts are the same. In both arenas, peacebuilders view conflict as an opportunity to approach problems and make decisions in ways that build the human community. To this end, they engage the parties in approaches that honor and call forth their fullest potential and invite the parties to recognize the needs and potential of others. These goals may be more difficult to accomplish with groups than with individuals. But in both settings, they help peacebuilders define their purpose and set their priorities in terms of criteria deeper than "getting a settlement."

The common denominator—and the biggest challenge—in both situations is the person of the peacebuilder, the one with the audacity and capacity to work in the terrain of other people's lives and communities with an agenda for transformation. Anyone who fails to recognize that this is a perilous agenda should not even think of trying to take it up. The line between transformation and imposition is narrow, and we have already begun to cross it when we think that we have what someone else needs.

Early in the book we said that transformation begins with a deep awareness of the uniqueness and intrinsic value of each human being. If people are truly unique, they are and always will be something of a mystery to others. No one else is capable of knowing with full certainty what other people need.

However, we know that the parties face a test that is often severe. Whether the conflict is interpersonal or intergroup, our role is to stand with the parties in that test and to help establish processes of interaction that support constructive responses. We encourage each party to reach for its fullest potential; we challenge each to recognize and honor the intrinsic worth of the other party; we facilitate processes of interaction that support these responses. If we attempt more than this—if, for example, we try to solve others' problems for them—we limit our transformative role, for transformation requires that the parties exercise their own abilities to solve problems.

To stand with others who are in struggle and pain, without responding in ways that limit the transformative potential of that situation for them, is one of the most difficult—and transformative—demands we can make of ourselves. We exercise our powers of recognition by truly seeing the pain and difficulty of others. At the same time, we test our own empowerment in persisting to stand in a place that is difficult. The task of peacebuilding then requires great transformation in the peacebuilder. For most peacebuilders, our own limits as less-than-transformed human beings prove to be a greater obstacle than our lack of technical skills.

Experience in mediating interpersonal conflicts develops skills essential for leadership in responding to group conflicts. Perhaps even more important, work in interpersonal conflicts moves us into a journey of personal transformation as peacebuilders. Every step in this personal journey advances our readiness to contribute to transformation in the larger web of the human community.

 The Jossey-Bass Web site (www.josseybass.com/peaceskills) provides numerous suggestions for designing a process for group and intergroup conflicts, for assessing community conflict, and for conducting large group dialogue.

APPLICATION EXERCISES

1. What moral and spiritual resources enable you as a peacebuilder to face the temptation to have control or power over other people? In an environment in which culture, race, attitudes, and beliefs divide people, what enables you to bridge the gulf between persons who are different from yourself? What blocks you from being a peacebuilder?

2. With one or two dialogue partners, share stories of when you have witnessed *bad* process. After hearing several accounts, see if these bad experiences would have been prevented by application of the principles of good process design outlined in the chapter. If not, formulate additional principles that address these failures.

3. Consider the following examples.

Example A

Outcome: A community service organization that needs additional space decides to build a new building rather than rent additional space nearby.

Process: The director of the organization decides that a new building is needed, finds a donor to fund it, and announces plans to build.

Example B

Outcome: In spite of reservations of some employees, two organizations doing similar work merge.

Process: A series of meetings are held involving key staff of the two organizations. In these joint meetings, they develop a series of guiding principles for a merger. The details of how to implement the principles are then worked out by a joint committee. The final proposal is ratified by boards and staffs in both organizations.

a. Which example represents bad process? _____

Why? _____

b. Which example represents good process? _____

Why? _____

c. What factors make a process good or bad?

d. Are there any drawbacks to the processes you described as good and advantages of those you described as bad?

e. What specific suggestions do you have for improving the processes in those selected as bad?

Chapter One

1.   The concept of empowerment has long been recognized by some media as central to the task of building peace. See, for example, Ron Kraybill and John Paul Lederach, "The Paradox of Popular Justice: A Practitioner's View," in Sally Engle Merry and Neal Milner (eds.), *The Possibility of Popular Justice: A Case Study of Community Mediation in the United States* (Ann Arbor: University of Michigan Press, 1995), pp. 357–378. But Robert A. Baruch Bush and Joseph P. Folger broke new ground in systematically applying the concept of empowerment to all phases of mediation in their book *The Promise of Mediation: Responding to Conflict Through Empowerment and Recognition* (San Francisco: Jossey-Bass, 1994).

Like theorists of moral development such as Carol Gilligan, Bush and Fo believe that human moral capacity increases as people learn two related but somewhat contradictory abilities: strengthening the self through *empowerment* and reaching beyond the self to relate to others, which these authors call *recognition*. Bush and Folger argue that a goal of human moral development (they call it "moral transformation") should guide mediators, not a preoccupation with particular outcomes such as getting an agreement. The task for mediators is merely to assist the parties to interact in ways that support them to become more empowered and to offer recognition to their opponents. While their argument may at points be simplistic and too narrowly focused on individual relationships, we find it compatible with our own approaches to mediation and to themes of empowerment and community we have developed elsewhere (see Kraybill and Lederach, "The Paradox of Popular Justice"). Because the twin categories of empowerment and recognition so elegantly capture the core intent of most of the activities we view as important in mediation, we use them as terms of reference in describing the larger purpose behind many skills described in this manual.

Chapter Two

1.   Ray Shonholtz, founder of the San Francisco Boards program, has written insightfully in this regard. See his essay, "What Mediation Training Says—or Doesn't Say—About the Ideology and Culture of North American Community-Justice Programs," in Sally Engle Merry and Neal Milner (eds.), *The Possibility of Popular Justice: A Case Study of Community Mediation in the United States* (Ann Arbor: University of Michigan Press, 1993), pp. 201–238.

Chapter Seven

1.   Roger Fisher and William Ury drew attention to this strategy in their widely read book, *Getting to Yes: Negotiating Agreement Without Giving In* (Boston: Houghton Mifflin, 1981). Fisher and Ury use slightly different terminology, referring to a party's demands as one's "position."

Chapter Eight

1.   The same dynamic applies in daily life in many situations. Parents who are overresponsible, for example, tend to raise children who are underresponsible and dependent. Clergy or community leaders who are overresponsible foster underresponsibility in others around them. The goal in any situation is to be *responsible,* performing the things that contribute to one's own well-being and that of others but not slipping into excesses of overresponsibility, doing for others things that they are quite capable of doing for themselves. Determining the meaning of responsibility is often difficult. Helping a three-year-old get dressed in the morning is probably responsible behavior for the parent. But helping a ten-year-old with the same task may be overresponsible and foster underresponsibility and dependence on the part of the child. As children grow, parents must change their own behavior in order to foster healthy responsibility in the child. This requires much thought and a willingness to experiment with behaviors that may at first bring complaints from the child. For more on the concept of overresponsibility and underresponsibility, see the writings of American family systems therapist Murray Bowen or the classic work by his student, Edwin Friedman, *Generation to Generation: Family Process in Church and Synagogue* (New York: Guilford Press, 1985).

Chapter Fourteen

1.   James Laue proposed that mediators view their role as advocates not of a particular party or outcome but of a particular process of interaction in his essay "Ethical Considerations in Choosing Intervention Roles," *Peace and Change*, 1992, 8(2–3), 30. For a critique of mediator "neutrality," see James Laue and Gerald Cormick, "The Ethics of Intervention in Community Disputes," in Gordan Bermant, Herbert C. Kelman, and Donald P. Warwick (eds.), *The Ethics of Social Intervention* (Washington, D.C.: Halsted Press, 1978), pp. 205–232.

APPENDIX

Additional Reading About Conflict Transformation

Augsburger, D. *Conflict Mediation Across Cultures: Pathways and Patterns.* Louisville, Ky.: Westminster/John Knox, 1992.

Bush, R.A.B., and Folger, J. P. *The Promise of Mediation: Responding to Conflict Through Empowerment and Recognition.* San Francisco: Jossey-Bass, 1994.

Fisher, R., Ury, W., and Patton, B. *Getting to Yes: Negotiating Agreement Without Giving In.* (2nd ed.) New York: Penguin Books, 1991.

Friedman, E. *Generation to Generation: Family Process in Church and Synagogue.* New York: Guilford Press, 1985. Excellent in applying concepts of family systems awareness to religious systems.

Lederach, J. P. *The Journey Toward Reconciliation.* Scottdale, Pa.: Herald Press, 1999.

McCollough, C. R. *Resolving Conflict with Justice and Peace.* New York: Pilgrim Press, 1991.

Mennonite Conciliation Service. *Mediation and Facilitation Training Manual: Foundations and Skills for Constructive Conflict Transformation.* (4th ed.) Akron, Pa.: Mennonite Central Committee, 2000. A comprehensive manual with substantial sections on mediation, group facilitation, decision making, conflict intervention, and theological perspectives. Packed with ideas, techniques, handouts, and many bibliographical suggestions.

Schock-Shenk, C., and Ressler, L. (eds.). *Making Peace with Conflict: Practical Skills for Conflict Transformation.* Scottdale, Pa.: Herald Press, 1999.

Schreiter, R. *The Ministry of Reconciliation: Spirituality and Strategies.* Maryknoll, N.Y.: Orbis Books, 1998.

Wink, W. *The Powers That Be: Theology for a New Millennium.* New York: Doubleday, 1998.

 Additional suggestions can be found at www.josseybass.com/peaceskills.

THE AUTHORS

RONALD S. KRAYBILL holds a bachelor's degree from Goshen College, a master's degree in divinity from Harvard Divinity School, and a doctorate in religious studies from the University of Cape Town. From 1979 to 1988, Kraybill was founding director of the Mennonite Conciliation Service based in Akron, Pennsylvania, and in this capacity worked with conflicts in family, community, business, neighborhood, and congregational settings and trained a large number of people in mediation skills. From 1989 to 1995, he served as director of training at the Centre for Conflict Resolution in Cape Town, South Africa. During the years of the South African political transition, he trained local, regional, and national leadership in negotiation and mediation skills and served as a training adviser to the National Peace Accord. Since 1995 Kraybill has been an associate professor in the Conflict Transformation Program at Eastern Mennonite University in Harrisonburg, Virginia, where he and his colleagues work with a network of partner organizations in the United States, Latin America, Africa, Asia, and Europe. From August 1999 to June 2000, Kraybill served as a visiting professor at the Henry Martyn Institute, an international center for interreligious dialogue and reconciliation in Hyderabad, India. In addition to many published essays, he has written *Repairing the Breach: Ministering in Community Conflict*, co-edited with Lynn Buzzard *Mediation: A Reader*, and edited *Training Manual for Conflict Transformation Skills*.

ALICE FRAZER EVANS was educated at Agnes Scott College, University of Edinburgh, and University of Wisconsin. She is the director of writing and research at Plowshares Institute and senior fellow at the Centre for Conflict Resolution in Cape Town, South Africa. A prolific case writer, she has focused on the development of international case studies, with special attention to the use of cases in conflict transformation training. Alice Evans is the founding executive director of an international association for case teaching. She is the co-author and editor of a number of books on global issues including *Christian Ethics: A Case Method Approach, Pastoral Theology from a Global Perspective,* and *Pedagogies for the Non-Poor.* She is a co-national director of a project on empowering for reconciliation with justice for which she developed curriculum material for civic and religious leaders in ten pilot project cities from Los Angeles to Philadelphia. Alice has taught, consulted, and trained case writers in workshops in Africa, Asia, Europe, Latin America, and North America. She is an elder and lay leader in the United Presbyterian Church. Her current teaching, research, and writing focus on U.S. cities, China, Indonesia, East Timor, and east and southern Africa.

ROBERT A. EVANS studied at Yale and the Universities of Edinburgh, Berlin, and Basel. He received his doctorate from Union Theological Seminary in New York. He is the author, co-author, editor of a dozen books, including *Globalization of Theological Education, Case Book for Christian Living,* and *Human Rights: A Dialogue Between the First and Third Worlds.* An ordained Presbyterian pastor, Bob Evans served as a professor in universities and seminaries in New York, Chicago, Uganda, Fiji, and Hartford. He currently serves as a senior fellow at the Centre for Conflict Resolution in Cape Town, South Africa. Bob is the founder and executive director of Plowshares Institute, which is committed to education, research, and dialogue for a more just, sustainable, and peaceful world community. He leads intensive traveling seminars for government, business, and religious leaders from Africa, Asia, and Latin America. He conducts national and international seminars on skills training in community conflict transformation on five continents. Bob co-directed with Alice Frazer Evans a pilot program for the Pew, Ford, and Kellogg Foundations in Philadelphia and Los Angeles on empowering for reconciliation with justice. This project, which has expanded to eight other cities in North America, equips multiethnic teams of religious and civic leaders to be proactive intervenors in community conflict situations. Bob and Alice Evans are currently developing projects in conflict transformation and sustainable development in East Timor, Hong Kong, Indonesia, Kenya, Uganda, and Zimbabwe.

ABOUT PLOWSHARES INSTITUTE

PLOWSHARES INSTITUTE WAS FOUNDED in 1981 to address systemic issues of injustice through education, research, and service. A nonprofit agency in partnership with an international advisory council and collaborative agencies on five continents, the Institute staff designs and implements pilot projects to promote a more just, sustainable, and peaceful world society. Pilot projects have included the Citizens of the World, Empowering for Reconciliation with Justice, Globalization of Theological Education, and Community Conflict Transformation (CCT).

The goal of community conflict transformation programs is to provide mediation skills training and curriculum material to equip civic, religious, and business leaders to work together in building just and more harmonious communities. For the past decade Plowshares staff members have been working with government and community leaders in Asia, Africa, and in ten North American cities from Los Angeles to Hartford in proactive approaches to community conflict. Multiethnic and multicultural teams of mediators trained in these programs have helped transform communities dealing with problems from community policing to public education. Workshop participants have also become trainers, equipping additional local leaders with mediation and transformation skills in East Timor, Hong Kong, Indonesia, Kenya, North America, South Africa, Uganda, and Zimbabwe.

Plowshares directors, Robert A. Evans and Alice Frazer Evans, are consultants and lead seminars for civic, business, academic, religious, and military leaders on five continents. The Evanses began developing a model for international immersion seminars in 1975. More than forty Plowshares seminars have brought together community and religious and leaders from North America with colleagues in Africa, Asia, Australia, Central Europe, and Latin America. The seminars not only build mutually beneficial international relationships, they also have a proven record of energizing participants to apply what they learn overseas to address local problems. Plowshares directly supports with volunteer service and funds a number of non-profit organizations in the developing world which share its vision.

The Evanses were founding members of the Association for Case Teaching and its co-executive directors for more than twenty-five years. Because of its potential for cooperative learning and for empowering people to draw on their own skills and experience to resolve dilemmas, the case method is a foundational pedagogy for Plowshares training in community conflict transformation.

Plowshares research, designed to share insights and promote the goals of pilot projects, is published in the form of case studies, articles, and a dozen books. The books include *Changing the Way Seminaries Teach; Christian Ethics: A Case Method Approach; The Globalization of Theological Education; Human Rights: A Dialogue Between the First and Third Worlds; Pastoral Theology from a Global Perspective*; and *Pedagogies for the Non-Poor*.

Peace Skills in Action: A Video for Community Conflict Transformation (CCT) Training and Interpretation

The twenty-minute video dramatically presents the need, vision, background, content, and consequences of Community Conflict Transformation training. This proactive approach to conflict intervention is illustrated by images of individuals and communities engaged in the training. The video also includes presentations on the impact of conflict transformation by mediators and trainers from Africa, Asia, and North America. This engaging video is designed to be used as an instrument to recruit workshop participants, to secure funding for the training, to clarify the approach, and to show CCT's global and local applications.

The video is available from Plowshares Institute, P.O. Box 243, Simsbury, CT 06070. Phone: 860/651–4304; Fax: 860/651–4305; e-mail: Plowshares@ hartsem.edu. Please consult the Plowshares's Web site for additional information: www.plowsharesinstitute.com.

ABOUT THE CONFLICT TRANSFORMATION PROGRAM

WELCOMING PEOPLE from all parts of the world and all religious traditions, the CTP is an outgrowth of the centuries-old Mennonite peace tradition rooted in values of nonviolence, social justice, public service, reconciliation, personal wholeness, and appreciation for diversity. Established in 1994 at Eastern Mennonite University in Harrisonburg, Virginia, the program builds on the extensive experience of Mennonites in the areas of disaster response, humanitarian relief, socio-economic development, conciliation, trauma healing, and restorative justice in exploring peaceful and creative responses to conflict.

Three closely related initiatives make up the CTP. An academic program offers a forty-two-credit-hour master's degree in conflict transformation for residential and limited-residential students, as well as a fifteen-hour-graduate certificate. Both are designed for persons with experience in conflict transformation or related areas, such as humanitarian assistance, community services, restorative justice, advocacy, human rights, or development activities, and who seek additional preparation in the field of conflict transformation. Students are encouraged to concentrate in one of six areas: conflict transformation and peacebuilding, restorative justice, mediation and facilitation, conflict transformation and the congregation, conflict transformation and organizational leadership, or conflict transformation and education. Since the work of peacebuilding is demanding, students are also encouraged to develop ethical, emotional, and spiritual resources to sustain them in long-term work in stressful situations. In 2000, seventy students from every region of the world enrolled and were taught by six core faculty and a larger number of adjunct faculty.

The Institute for Justice and Peacebuilding (IJP) is the applied practice and research component of the Conflict Transformation Program. It provides direct services in peacebuilding in the form of trainings, consultancies, peace-process design, conciliation, mediation, and action-oriented research to religious, academic, intergovernmental, and community organizations worldwide. IJP is staffed by associates who, as practitioner/scholars, have broad experience as educators and trainers in conflict transformation and as practitioners of peacebuilding. With extensive experience in diverse cultural environments, they are in the forefront of culturally contextualized approaches to the training and practice of conflict transformation. Through links with strategic partners in Africa, Asia, and Latin America and with practitioners engaged in peacebuilding worldwide, the Institute for Justice and Peacebuilding provides a connection between current practice and advances in theory and concept.

The Summer Peacebuilding Institute is held annually in May and June for academic and non-academic participants who seek an intensive training experience with diverse colleagues from around the world. Participants choose from among fifteen seven-day courses in conflict transformation, mediation and facilitation, trauma healing, restorative justice, and other topics. In 2000, 141 participants attended from forty-five countries and seventeen U.S. states, representing seven religious traditions and twenty Christian denominations, with almost equal numbers of women and men. Participants were affiliated with religious and humanitarian agencies, with nongovernmental, governmental, and intergovernmental organizations, as well as with peacebuilding and conflict transformation programs, restorative justice organizations, and academic institutions.

For more information and access to additional related Web sites, visit the Conflict Transformation Program Web site at: www.emu.edu/ctp/ctp.html.

Conflict Transformation Program, Eastern Mennonite University, Harrisonburg, VA, 22802. Phone: (540) 432–4490; Fax: (540) 432–4449; email: ctprogram@emu.edu.

INDEX

CPSIA information can be obtained
at www.ICGtesting.com
Printed in the USA
JSHW050216021222
34003JS00005B/9

9 780787 947996